Time Management Hacks

How to Stop Procrastinating, Increase Productivity and Get More Done in Less Time

Andrea Chase Harper

responsibility or liability for any third party products or opinions. Third party product manufacturers have not sanctioned this book, nor does the author receive any compensation from said manufacturers for sharing information regarding their products.

Table of Contents

Introduction

There never seems to be enough time.

You wake up. You rush to work. You hurry from task to task. You find yourself bouncing to and from meetings all day long. You then rush back home and race to handle chores, dinner and the kids. By the end of the day, you rush to spend any precious minutes left doing something relaxing. And finally, hurry to bed and do it all over again the next day.

Sound familiar?

Between work, chores, commuting, and sleep, it can feel like you have no free time in your day. Maybe you plan to work on hobbies on the weekend, but you're too tired to get anything done before the next week. This can be frustrating, and unfortunately it affects many people in their day-to-day lives. Poor time management skills can leave you feeling drained. But like any skill, time management can be learned, and the more you practice it, the better you'll get. When you develop your skills, you'll be able to make more time for hobbies, spend more time with family, and have a more enjoyable day-to-day life.

Throughout this book, you'll learn step by step how to bring balance to your life. You'll learn methods to prioritize tasks, manage meetings, focus, and how to add self-care to your day. These methods will help you make time management a regular habit. You won't just be making checklists and forgetting about them. You are going to learn how to develop lasting patterns of action that you can integrate into your day. You're learning a skill, not simply a trick. If you follow all the recommendations here, you'll find yourself more organized than you ever thought you could be.

I used to struggle a lot with time management. It was hard for me to make it to events on time, get assignments done and find time to spend with my family. Living life with that much rushing makes you feel like a snowball, constantly rolling downhill, your to-do list growing bigger and bigger as you struggle along your path. Through reflection, I was able to develop critical time management skills. This was life changing, to say the least. I don't wake up stressed anymore. I don't speed to appointments and work. I don't stay up late doing chores. I don't have to choose between work and family. I have created time for hobbies. I even have free time where I can relax, watch TV, and simply take a deep breath. It bears repeating, but time management has drastically improved my well-being.

And, now, I'm taking what I've learned on this journey and giving it to you. The advice contained in these chapters is what gave me the ability to change my life for the better. I want you to have this change, too.

With these new skills, you'll be able to expand your personal capacities in ways you've never before experienced. You will be able to fit many tasks into your day, week, month, and even year. You'll also have better self-esteem. It feels good to be able to balance your life perfectly; a confidence boost is natural. You'll also gain free time and time to spend with the people who are important to you. Friends and family will play a bigger role in your life. This may sound too good to be true, but it's not. With hard work and self-discipline, you can reap the rewards of a perfectly managed lifestyle.

Time management isn't just a feel-good skill. There have been numerous studies over the years that show that time management skills have real, empirical benefits for people. A 2019 study found that university students got better grades and had reduced symptoms of anxiety when they had proper time management skills (Adams & Blair, 2019). A separate study from 2015 both found the same results as the aforementioned one, and it found that students with poor time management skills were less likely to perform well in their classes. This study also found that students who measured their studying by time spent reading, instead of measuring their actual information taken in, did not do as well as their peers, even if they spent more time studying (Khan & Nasrullah, 2015). Time management isn't just doing more things or doing things faster. It's learning how to make your time valuable. There are potent benefits to learning how to properly manage your time, as you will soon see for yourself.

Chapter by chapter, you'll learn how to sort your priorities so you don't let things slip through the cracks. You'll learn how to form permanent routines that stick with you for more than a couple days. You'll be able to manage your meetings and day-to-day interactions that seem to just sap time right out of your schedule. You'll learn organization skills that will help you get the most use out of every minute. Finally, you'll learn how to do all these things without forgetting about your own physical and mental health. As you put the principles in this book into practice, you will develop the ability to spend your time wisely, making efficient choices and reducing stress.

You may have picked up this book because you find yourself reflecting on all the things you could have time for if you could just manage to reorganize your life. Maybe you want to spend more time with your family. Maybe you want to practice a hobby, like learning to play an instrument or finally getting into gardening. Maybe you simply want more free time to relax or meditate. Now that you have this book, you can start making those changes. It doesn't matter how long it took you to get to this point to realize that something in your life needs to change. You can change it now. The sooner you change your behaviors, the sooner you can start checking off those long neglected boxes and those forgotten hobbies.

This book will give you all the tools you need to become a master of time management. There's only one thing this book can't give you.

That thing is action. Reading is passive. Wanting is passive. Change is active. If you truly want to change your behavior, then you need to start acting. Get moving. Read this book and learn what you need to do, then go do it.

Take note of the person you are now. At the end of this journey, you'll be someone different.

Someone better.

Chapter 1: When Work is Long and Time is Fleeting

The way we spend the time we are given defines the kind of lifestyle we lead. In the same manner that people who procrastinate fall behind at work, those who spend hours on the same task are considered just as inefficient. The key to being a promising professional is not how long you spend working, but how much work you can productively complete within a given time frame. The more you accomplish, the more successful you are.

Beware of Cognitive Dissonance

For the average employee, they each have their own idea of what they would like to achieve. Some people are happy only doing the tasks delegated to them, others actively seek out more things to do, and a few engage in fierce competition to make their way to the top. It does not matter what your prerogative at work is, failing to maintain a professional approach can reflect negatively on your career, no matter how talented you are. If you desire to be a certain type of employee, yet consistently see yourself not completing tasks on a daily basis simply because time is never by your side, then you may experience cognitive dissonance.

A condition that causes stress, it stems from a pronounced failure to effectively manage your time and progress in your career. In worst cases, the stress and anxiety can lead to both serious mental and physical deterioration of health. But why do some people fall into this trap? Here are the most common reasons:

1) **Impatience:** Not everybody is blessed with the power of patience. Many people, especially if you already have issues with anxiety, tend to want immediate responses. What this creates is a response in the gratification center in the brain that can now assess its next steps in dealing with any situation. For a naturally impatient person, they can produce sloppy work, wait till the last minute before they get productive, or force themselves into a corner because their impatience is affecting the quality of their work.

2) **The Ability to Predict:** Strategic time management takes into consideration the capacity of an individual to predict the events of the day. But random variables such as surprise meetings, surprise deadlines or minor hassles at work can throw off an individual's ability to manage time. Without the necessary qualities of flexibility and adaptability, surviving in a workplace environment is complicated.

3) **Over-Estimation of One's Ability:** You may think that it takes you fifteen minutes to finish writing a report at work, so you do something unrelated until you have just fifteen minutes left to write the report. What you had failed to take into consideration was the time it would take to do the research for the report or format the document. You suddenly find yourself realizing that you actually need half an hour, and if you had just not wasted your time, you could have finished work within the deadline. What you did was over estimate your abilities, when all you had to do was take the time to do the job well.

4) **Procrastination:** People tend to leave what they can do to the last minute, and this can happen because of various reasons. Some people believe that by waiting, they give themselves time to think about the project, while others want to perform research. But primarily, people just want to find excuses. A large portion of the people waiting will not, in fact even think

about the project until the deadline appears. By the time they do put the work in, the process becomes a rush job and the project never reaches the height it could have.

How Productivity Lags On The Job

Mismanaged time is often a reflection on the person's lifestyle. A person who is not properly managing their time at work are very likely making those same mistakes in other areas of their lives as well. They may not be good at taking care of themselves. They are also more likely to either skip meals altogether or rely on a steady diet of takeout.

Basically, the ability to decently manage time is something that is usually embedded in people during their development phase, primarily in school. It is not unusual to find people who used to hand in assignments regularly during their student years suddenly finding themselves dumbfounded at being unable to complete simple tasks at work. While you are bound to come across a few lazy souls in the search to find the unproductive, it is simplistic to assume that they form the broader category of those that badly manage time. But what are the most common reasons that explain why people are unproductive at work?

Here are the four most common culprits of productivity lag:

1) **Feeling Overwhelmed:** One of the biggest reasons people bring up is that they feel overwhelmed by all the tasks they have to accomplish on a daily basis. Some even feel stifled by everyday tasks such as meal preparation or even taking a bath. The reason behind this is that these people only see the day ahead as a checklist of all that needs to be completed instead of spreading out the day with an achievable distribution of work. Rather they build up stress wondering how they will complete everything, These people convince themselves that everything needs to be finished *now* and in

doing so, push themselves into a corner where they feel too intimidated to do anything at all.

2) **Lack of Energy:** If you feel that you do not have the energy to finish the task or feel sleepy and lethargic on a daily basis, then your work performance is bound to be affected. It is important to get a health check up to cross out any possible underlying health problems that may be causing this. However, even a bad daily diet can cause lethargy. In addition, mental fatigue can also cause this kind of lethargy. If you find yourself constantly stressing out, then you will be inviting in other health issues. Productive people typically engage in more healthy ways of eating, including balanced meals and nutrition.

3) **Focus:** The ability to focus is directly proportional to success. If you are not invested in what you do, then you may find yourself easily distracted. Of course there are various situations that can cause you to lose your attention, but the key to remember is that while you are at work, you have an obligation to give your employer the time that they are investing in you to provide. A professional work ethic requires the ability to focus on your work when it is needed.

4) **Work Satisfaction:** At some point in our lives, most of us end up working in a profession we are not particularly interested in. Not everybody can be rock stars or astronauts. Working at a job you are good at while not enjoying any other aspect of your life can be frustrating. You may love the office and hate the job or the other way around. There are various things you can do to make a change, starting with deciding which aspect of your life you are willing to compromise on. Do you want to give up your job and look for a new one? Or do you want to

keep working for that promotion you really want. The key here is to figure out what you really want from your career. Higher work satisfaction will lead to greater focus and overall productivity.

Bad time management is often intentional. The only way to stop yourself from not being able to manage it is to make a conscious decision to do the opposite. Luckily, time management is a skill that can be learned, and there is no need for you to compromise on your career.

Chapter 2: Prioritizing

Why is it that when discussing time management methods, priority selection is one of the first topics? Before we dive into this subject, I want you to do an experiment with me. Imagine that in front of you are a few interesting objects on a table. A cup, ping pong balls, beads from a necklace, and sand. Your task is to fill the cup to the brim with as many of these objects as possible. You have to use each type of object when filling the cup. Try to think this scenario through, or even recreate it to see different methods of filling the cup. What do you start with? How much of each object do you use? How would you prioritize this task?

Imagine starting with the smallest object, then working your way to the largest. This would surely help the cup to fill up faster, right? When you try this, you fill the cup as much as you can with sand, then add the beads. But, wait, there isn't any room for the beads. The sand takes up too much space and the beads just sit at the top. It's even harder to balance the ping pong balls on top of the beads. Try the beads first. Now, you can pour in the sand. It fits through the gaps. But the ping pong balls are still stuck without a place to go. Put the ping pong balls in first. Now, the beads can fit between those. Then, add the sand, and it will fill in all the other gaps. The cup is full and you used each object to fill it up. You could even add a bit of water if you wanted to as it would soak into the sand.

When you learn to correctly prioritize, you learn how to fit a larger number of tasks into the same amount of time. It can be difficult to determine what tasks are ping pong balls and which are sand. If you're already stressed or anxious, it's even harder to tell what tasks are more important than others.

There are, however, a few useful methods for weighing tasks to see which ones are higher or lower level. First, assess their long-term impact. In a month, in six months, in a year, which task or goal will be more important? Which is more likely to have a greater impact on your life? This question will help you find your ping pong balls. Tasks and goals that affect you long-term should be put into action sooner rather than later.

Second, assess the urgency of the tasks. Yes, studying for your final will be more impactful in the future than doing your lab homework, but your lab is due in two days and your final is in two weeks. You can put the lab first. This question helps you find your beads. You'll still need time for smaller things, but maybe you can put a bigger priority aside briefly.

Third, ask yourself if the task is a *need* or a *must*. A lot of your prioritization skills will come from asking yourself this question and it will help you identify your sand. If you are strapped for time, you should be filling your cup with the least amount of sand possible, because you'll always have room for it here and there, and the more sand you use, the less room you have for your most important tasks.

Once you have your tasks categorized, you can begin making your to-do list. Writing things down to keep track of them is one of the best ways to force our brains to come to terms with the actual scope of tasks at hand (Chunn, 2017). If you're anxious or stressed, tasks can seem overly daunting or excessively simple. This can cause you to misinterpret which tasks are a priority. Simply writing your tasks down can reduce that anxiety and stress, so that you can go about your tasks without those emotional biases (Masicampo & Baumeister, 2011). However, it's not enough to just write a list with some checkmarks on it. You may even have experience with this, and have written off lists because they don't seem to work for you. It's actually very likely that your workflow would improve with a list, just not the kind you've been making.

There are a few ways to make your to do list actually work (O'Donovan, 2013). First and foremost is prioritization. Make a physical marker on your list of what tasks are most to least important. You could use color, numbers, or even make several different lists. Whatever way you choose, make sure it's obvious what tasks you need to get done first. Second, be active. It isn't enough to write a list on a post-it note and then forget about it. Look back at your list throughout the day and make sure you are checking off tasks in the correct order. Your list is not decoration, it's a tool. Third, go back and evaluate your performance. Remember that practice makes permanent, not perfect. If you want to start learning how to manage your tasks, you need to reflect on the lists you make and evaluate whether or not they were true or helpful. Did you correctly assign priorities this week? Did you actively engage with your list? Take your evaluation into account and change how you make your next list. Each time you do this, you will get better at making to-do lists.

The next skill you need to develop is shaping your time. Once you have your tasks laid out and ordered, you need to block out time to complete each one. This is also a very important facet of prioritizing. Without blocks, it is much more difficult to determine your time. Blocking your time also helps to keep you focused (Rampton, 2019). To block out your time, sit down and think through your day. Using your to do list, estimate how long each task will take. Make sure you overestimate instead of underestimating how much time you'll actually need. When you overestimate, and you save yourself some time, you can do extra work or have more time to relax. If you underestimate and end up going over your block, that will lead to stress and reduced productivity. Block your day so that you are focusing on one task at a time, and are giving it your full attention until it is time to move on. Try to put your most difficult or highest priority work at times when you are more productive, usually in the morning. You can save easier work for less productive times like right after lunch.

When you block your time correctly, your calendar should look like a quilt of different tasks. At first glance, it looks like you have no free time in your day. What's actually happening is that you have assigned a task to every hour of your work day. It's much easier to focus when you arrange your day like this. It also prevents you from trying to multitask. We are, as a species, physically incapable of multitasking (Kubu & Machado, 2017). If it feels like you are, you are really shifting your attention rapidly between two things. You can prove this to yourself by trying to listen to a podcast while writing an email. You will end up missing words on one of those to think about the words of the other. This is also what makes distracted driving so dangerous. Trying to multitask, or even thinking about future tasks while you are working on another one, shifts your concentration at the expense of your productivity. Blocking your time makes it so you can completely concentrate on one thing, then methodically shift your thoughts to another.

When you block your time, you need to add room for error. An airtight time block is almost as useless as not making one at all. You can't predict the future. You can't be certain how long a task will take, how many emails you'll get in a day, how long a meeting will last, and much more. There are dozens of factors throughout our days that influence how we spend our time. Trying to control all of them will be fruitless. When you block your time, plan out reactive tasks. These are tasks you were not expecting to do that are suddenly higher priority than the ones on your list. Give yourself blocks that are specifically for unexpected jobs. You don't need to do those things at the exact time the block is scheduled. These reactive blocks are place holders for when the unexpected happens. You can safely spend your time working on the new task at a moment's notice, and still have time in your day for your normal work.

For example, say I always have a reactive block from 2:30-3:00pm every day. That does not mean that every day at 2:30pm, I am sitting at my desk waiting for a new task. It means that any time during the day, I can take half an hour to work on something my boss asks me to do that I wasn't planning on doing. If I'm never asked to do an extra task, I simply finish work half an hour early.

This over-preparedness is a habit I learned early on in my childhood. My dad would always encourage us to over prepare. I used to think he had Mary Poppins pockets. Whenever we needed something when we were out, be it a pen or paper or a tissue or the weather report from the newspaper, he had it on him. I do this now too, thanks to him, sometimes to my own detriment. My purse can get really heavy sometimes. I was always the mom friend in high school because I had meds, writing utensils, and feminine products on me at all times. I use this skill now when I'm trying to manage my time. Blocking for reactive tasks is the planning version of always having a pen on me. I highly recommend you adopt this attitude, too. Just make sure you have a backpack or purse with sturdy straps.

When you block your work, you should focus not only on the actual tasks but on the type of work you'll be doing. There are two types of focusing when we work. These types are deep work and shallow work. Blocking your time lets you determine when you will be doing each type, making it infinitely easier to switch. Shallow work consists of tasks that don't require full concentration or that can be done without too much brain power. Shallow work includes brief, routine communication such as emails or weekly progress meetings. You need to concentrate, but you aren't reinventing the wheel. Deep work involves creating, thinking, and innovating. Writing and programming are good examples of deep work.

When you create your time blocks, you should block for both the specific task at hand and which type of work it is. Try to keep the times at which you engage in different types of work consistent throughout your week. If you can focus more in the morning, reserve two hours then for deep work, with another block of shallow work afterwards. Don't double up on deep work, it's mentally challenging and you'll tire yourself out very quickly. You should also purposely include blocks in your day that don't have an assigned task but are reserved for shallow work. This is where you can place any extra work such as catching up on emails and IMs. Remember that when you engage in deep work, you will want to spare yourself from any potential distractions, so these small "free space" blocks are where you can put those fleeting tasks.

Your first work day that you block out will not be perfect. It takes lots of self-awareness to create a schedule that works for you. There are apps and calendars online or for your phone that can help you block out your work day, but every template will need tweaking. This is what makes reflection so important. Just like with your to-do lists, you need to ask yourself what does and doesn't work in your blocks. You can also reach out to coworkers or management to let them know that you are blocking your workday. This can help you stick to your self-assigned blocks. For example, if you set your email to auto-reply when you are in a deep work session, it will be easier for you to concentrate, and your coworkers are less likely to be frustrated over a seemingly delayed response.

Your blocks can also encompass a day, instead of a portion of an hour. If your workflow requires several meetings, you could set aside a day specifically for those meetings. Then, you can focus your attention for that whole day on meetings and interpersonal collaboration. This again helps prevent multitasking. You should also be including creativity in your blocks. Deep work usually includes, but is not exclusively, creative. You should add blocks throughout the week that emphasize creating. Whatever field you are in, creativity can enhance your performance. Bringing new ideas to the table helps you to get more things done. It can also help you deepen your understanding of that topic. Finally, make sure you are including breaks and personal time in your day. Give yourself room to breathe. It's very difficult to focus intently for two hours without looking up from your screen. This is why overestimating your time is so important; it gives you free time. Free time is not a waste of time. If you find yourself daydreaming or staring into space, that's a sign that you are losing your concentration battery. Take a short break and reset yourself. Thirty minutes of unbroken concentration with a five-minute break is much better than an hour of on-and-off focus.

Your prioritization will include assigning importance to tasks, creating an ordered to-do list, and blocking your time for both tasks and types of focus. When you manage to do all these things correctly, you will create a rhythm in your workday like poetry. However, this will take lots of practice and development of self-awareness. Trial and error is your friend. You will be learning by doing. Some people prefer to read and study in order to learn. It's ok if you are intimidated by these techniques. Fear of failure is normal, but you can, and must, learn to overcome it. If you are uncomfortable with the learning by doing method, try to identify other things in your life that you have to learn by doing. Tasks such as riding a bike, tying a new knot, and cooking must be learned by trial and error. You already have practice utilizing this skill, you now need to bring it to your workplace.

If you are still anxious about changing your daily routine this much, be open about your journey with your peers and managers. They will be supportive of you on your path to self-improvement, and communication will only make them more understanding. The more you try something and fail, the more you learn. In this case, you will be learning about yourself. The self-awareness you are going to develop is going to make your skills at time assessment and blocking much better, but they will also help with the next step in learning time management: routine development.

Chapter 3: Build Your Routines

A routine is incredibly important. It's the next level of prioritizing and blocking. When you manage to find a routine that works for you, you'll be able to practice it so regularly that it becomes a habit. Then, you can move through your routine without actively thinking about it, freeing up mental space. This is, of course, much easier said than done.

Forming a routine is hard to do. If you've tried it and failed to come up with something permanent, you may have dismissed them altogether. Maybe you think you hate routines, that the repetitive nature of them drives you mad. There are some underlying reasons for those feelings. When you create a routine the right way, you can be certain you will have fantastic results.

Routines can look like different things for different people. Not just in the way they're made up, but in the actual definition itself. For some, routine means that even without blocking their day or scheduling their activities, they are doing the same things at the same time every day. They wake up at the same time, have the same breakfast, the same morning hygiene routine and go to work listening to the same radio station. These types of routines are the traditional idea of a routine: rigid and repetitive. But a routine doesn't have to be this stiff. If it works for you, that's fantastic! Keep going! But for some, trying out this kind of routine only leads to feelings of defeat when they can't stick to it.

I've found that an alternative definition of routine is helpful in this situation. For me, a routine isn't necessarily repetition; it's scheduling. I wake up and start my morning routine. I eat breakfast, though what that breakfast consists of changes periodically. I go through my hygiene routine and sometimes I change it up. Maybe one day I'm just not feeling makeup, so it's not part of my routine on that particular day. I try to make exercise a routine, too. But I don't expect to exercise every single day, let alone do the same exercise, like running during each workout. I listen to my body and mood and decide from there. Maybe one day I'm super energetic so I do some dance cardio. Maybe the next day I'm not feeling it at all, and I have to push myself to do five minutes of stretches. If I expected myself to follow the first definition of routine, I would be starting my day with feelings of shame and disappointment. Instead, I use self-awareness to make a generalized routine that allows for flexibility. Working out three times a week is still a routine. Planning your dinners on weekdays but not the weekend is still a routine. If you've had trouble following a strict routine in the past, try to adopt this flexibility into your mindset.

In order to develop your own personal routine, you need to figure out what works for your own personality. You need to develop self-awareness. This is a skill that takes lots of focus and practice. You may find it uncomfortable at first, like exercising a muscle you never have before.

Self-awareness is a skill we all have the capacity to develop, but are rarely ever taught. When you exercise proper self-awareness, you are able to understand the sources of your feelings, better interpret the conditions around you, and can contribute easier to changing your emotional responses to those conditions. I've developed self-awareness skills throughout the years that I use to regulate my emotions and control the environment around me. For example, say one day I am much more irritable than usual. My patience is wearing thin quickly. I'm easily annoyed and I'm just feeling angry about everything. I can use self-awareness skills to do a few things. First, I can realize that I'm feeling these emotions and be accepting of them.

If I notice myself getting snappy, I can ask myself what I'm actually feeling. I may be feeling anger or pain and haven't realized it. Once I identify this, I can ask myself why. With practice, it is easier to come up with possible solutions. I simply know myself better. Maybe I failed to achieve a goal earlier that week. Maybe I read the news and saw something that was upsetting. It could just be my time of the month. Whatever the cause, identifying it means I can then address it. I can reflect on that goal and adjust my expectations. I can read a book or take a warm bath. I can't always identify why I'm feeling an emotion, but the more I practice, the faster I can recognize it.

Self-awareness plays an enormous role in perfecting your time management skills. You will see it mentioned frequently in this book and in your self-improvement journey as a whole. There are three layers of self-awareness (Manson, 2018). Let's go over each one in depth.

The first layer is awareness of your actions. If you're new to self-awareness, it can be hard to realize when you are doing things that indicate different emotions. You may be reaching for your phone more often when you should be working. Before you can ask yourself why you are doing that, you need to be able to recognize that you are doing it in the first place. Journaling and writing things down are excellent ways to develop this skill. You should take time at the end of each day to reflect on your actions. What did you do well? What do you wish you had done? Where is there room for improvement?

These questions help you practice recognition of your actions. Mindfulness activities also deepen this skill. Meditation is a great way to improve your mindfulness. It helps you to actively notice your thoughts so that you aren't passively experiencing them. Passivity is the enemy of progress in this endeavor, and you should do your best to be actively moving and thinking throughout your day. Try, as you build your self-awareness skills, to avoid going on autopilot through your day.

The second layer is discovering how you feel. Once you have your actions down, you can start to dissect why you are doing them and what their consequences are. If you are acting impatient, you may be feeling mad. If you are acting generous, it may make you feel happy. This may seem elementary, but while it's easy to explain, it's very hard to do. This takes tons of practice. We aren't used to analyzing the reasons for our day to day actions. It will take a long time to get used to analyzing yourself like this. You'll start with more obvious emotions and actions. Once you can identify those, you'll be able to figure out more complex emotions. The final stage of this layer is understanding sequences of events. When you can properly recognize your emotions and your responses to them, you'll be able to understand yourself, your interactions with others, and what methods of time management work best for you. This is a skill that takes a long time to develop and is impossible to perfect. You'll be practicing it every day and you'll get better at it every time you do.

The final layer is understanding what you don't understand. It's the Socratic Paradox, "I know that I know nothing" (Messerly, 2019). To put it simply, it means that you are aware that you don't know everything. It's accepting that self-awareness is never perfect. More than that, it is the ability to recognize where you have gaps in your knowledge. To know where you can next focus for improvement. This concept can get nebulous. It may sound easy to understand. Maybe you can even think of examples for yourself while reading this. The reason that this is the final layer is that it requires you to develop the others first. If you have never worked on your self-awareness, then of course you can think of ways to improve it. The trick is to be able to think of them after a long time of personal exploration. Before you think you're on the final layer, it should feel like, no matter how much time you spend developing your self-awareness, you just can't figure out enough. This is because of the Dunning-Kruger effect (Cherry, 2019).

The Dunning-Kruger effect is a phenomenon in which the more a person knows about a subject, the less they think they know. Those who know very little about the subject tend to think they know more than some experts do. This is often used to explain why science denial occurs, but it can apply just as easily to self-awareness. If you have never practiced self-awareness before, but you feel like you could easily understand what you don't know about yourself, you're overestimating your knowledge. It's not a bad thing; practically everyone does this. But keep yourself in check and practice before you assume.

You can use self-awareness to develop your own personal routine. Figure out whether you like the strict or flexible types of routines better. The only way to truly figure this out is trial and error. Give yourself at least a week to try each type of routine, and it should be clear which you prefer. Next, just like you set priorities for your work tasks, set priorities for your routine tasks. Is it more important to wake up on time and have your coffee, or to sleep in and skip breakfast? The answers are different for everyone. Go through your daily schedule and ask yourself these questions. Write down the answers. At the end of a week, reflect on what you've written and evaluate what kind of routine you should make for yourself. Then test it out and continue writing and reflecting. You don't need to be an aspiring author to journal. These can be as simple as a few scribbled bullet points.

The point of writing your findings down is so you can correctly remember them when you go to reflect, instead of misremembering. We tend to remember negative things more than positive ones (Warner, 2007). Without writing things down, it's very easy to incorrectly evaluate your results. Correct evaluation is a key to self-awareness.

As you move through this process, you will probably find yourself tempted to be distracted. It can be incredibly easy to change your mind when your routine isn't yet a habit. We've all looked down at our phones when we should be working. This is natural. But there's a point where these distractions become time wasters, not attention refreshers. The self-awareness you develop will also tell you when you need a break versus when you want a break. If you find yourself taking breaks when you want them, not just when you need them, you're wasting your own time. You can manage this both by developing your self-awareness, and with a few tricks. First, make sure the only devices that you have access to while you are working are for work only. If you don't need your phone, put it out of sight. If you don't need social media, you can use a browser extension to temporarily block those websites. Second, try to give your mind nowhere to go while you are working. If you are engaged in a deep work task, this won't be too hard. If you're working on a shallow focus task, this is more difficult. You can put on music in the background. Try to use things without words, like movie soundtracks or classical music. This makes sure that you're not multitasking. You can also have some nice visuals near you that you can control. For example, I like to have a muted video up of someone playing a sport I like in the corner of my screen. You could use a livestream of animals or a picture you like.

Now, if my brain wants to zone out, I will keep my eyes on my computer screen instead of off in the distance. My work is right next to that video, so it's miles easier to snap my attention back to the task at hand.

Your blocking and prioritizing should help you to eliminate most of these time-wasting tendencies. In the beginning, it may not work as efficiently as you'd like. If you're having a lot of trouble with paying attention, you can also work on your self-discipline skills. Remind yourself, frequently, what you are doing and why. Remind yourself which task you're working on, what level of importance it is, when it's due. Have a post-it note stuck to your monitor or something very close to you that reminds you to refer back to those priorities. When you are constantly answering these questions for yourself, they get easier and easier to answer. Eventually, you'll find yourself answering them without asking. Instead of browsing social media for too long and then asking yourself, "Wait, what was I doing?" your subconscious thoughts will be telling you "I am doing x task because y" without you needing to kickstart that thought. Self-discipline is very similar to self-awareness in this way. Remember that breaks are not only good but necessary. You shouldn't be avoiding breaks. You should be avoiding unplanned and unneeded breaks. If you find you can't hold your attention to one thing for more than a few minutes, that's a sign you need a break. If it happens once an hour, you can work to minimize those attention drops.

A great place to start when you're building routines is to set daily goals. Goals can help us hold ourselves accountable. Learning how to set reasonable, achievable goals will help you develop self-awareness and will contribute to a sense of self-satisfaction. There are two types of goals you can set for yourself: mastery and performance (Riopel, 2019). Mastery goals involve testing your own personal skill or mastery of a subject. Striving to get an A in a class is a mastery goal. Performance goals compare your own success to others. Being the top salesman of the month is a performance goal. There are also two subsets of goals: avoidance and approach (Riopel, 2019).

Avoidance goals involve setting your goal target so that you avoid a negative outcome. You can set a mastery-avoidance goal by determining a grade you don't want in a class and then trying to get a grade higher than that. A performance-avoidance goal might be trying to do better than a specific coworker. Approach goals are framed so that the task is accomplished when you meet a bar. You could set a performance-approach goal by trying to set a record for fastest sprinter on your team. A mastery-approach goal is trying to get a 95% or higher on your midterm. Performance and mastery goals can be either avoidance or approach. Understanding these principles will help you mold your idea of daily goals. Say your goal is to finish work an hour earlier every day. Frame that goal around these four types. Since you are trying to do something compared to your own personal skill, it's a mastery goal. You are also trying to cut time from your work day and avoid working an extra hour. That's avoidance, so that makes this goal a mastery-avoidance goal. Now that you know that, you are better equipped to decide what angle to approach this from. From a mastery angle, you can try to improve your skill in some work-related field. Maybe you could increase your typing speed. For avoidance, you are trying to jump over a hurdle. You could start with a smaller hurdle, like fifteen minutes, and increase from there. Try to always form your goals around these approaches.

To make your daily goals, start by deciding what you want. This want could be based on the next week, or month, or even year. Say that, by the end of the year, you want to increase your typing speed by twenty words per minute. Now, break that goal down into smaller parts. You can use numerical metrics, such as wanting to increase your typing by five words per minute each month. You could also use more subjective measurements, such as decreasing your error rate when typing, or learning to type without looking at the keyboard. Now, break those goals down and plan out what methods you will need to accomplish them. You can practice writing as many words as you can in ten minutes, or type with a piece of paper over your hands for half the day.

However you choose to accomplish your goal, you should have something tangible to strive towards every day. Each day, add the goal practice to your daily routine. Block out time for it and make sure that when you engage with your goal, you are actively reminded of its purpose. It doesn't need to be a huge part of your day. These daily goals should help you to gradually accomplish what is too time consuming to achieve in fewer sittings.

You can also set daily goals that are less grandiose. Your daily goals can serve a large number of purposes. They could even be as simple as wanting to get more work done on that day. They can change from day to day and week to week. The true significance of setting and achieving daily goals is the confidence boost they give you. Researches in the 1990s found that setting goals daily is highly correlated with workplace performance. For example, people who set and attain daily goals that are sufficiently challenging are better performing than their peers who do not do so (Riopel, 2019). They found that a good goal has several aspects. Goals that do not have these characteristics risk being unhelpful or even hindering to progress. Goals need to be clear. You need to set daily goals that are not ambiguous in their outcomes. Responding to "enough" emails is an unclear goal. Responding to ten emails is a clear goal. Goals also need to be challenging. If you set the bar too low, you won't benefit from a sense of accomplishment when you complete it. Since that bar is different for everyone, finding the right amount of challenge takes trial and error. Goals need to be backed by personal commitment. When you set a goal, try your hardest to achieve it. Don't give yourself a get out of jail free card. If you get into the habit of not committing to your goals, they will lose meaning and you'll risk losing out on a powerful self-improvement tool. Make sure the complexity of your goal matches your tasks. If you set a goal to learn how to master French cooking, but you have trouble making pancakes, the complexity of your goal doesn't match the complexity of the tasks you'll be undertaking. Try to take it easy on yourself. Balance is healthy.

Last but not least, goals need to be reflected upon. Just like with routines and to do lists, if you aren't reflecting on and adjusting your goals, you won't learn how to set them properly, and they won't provide you any benefit.

So far, you've learned how to make to-do lists, prioritize tasks, develop self-awareness, routines, and goals. You may now have more questions than answers. I keep telling you that practice is necessary to develop those skills, but how do you actually do that?

These topics can seem very abstract, so before we move on, let's practice them on a smaller scale: in meetings.

Chapter 4: Manage Meetings

Many skills have macro and micro aspects. Expertise in one does not always mean expertise in the other. A high stakes stock investor may have trouble budgeting their income. A person could be excellent at identifying metaphor and meaning in a poem but unable to master spelling and grammar in their own writing. Someone who learns a language in a classroom probably has great micro skills such as definitions of words and verb conjugations, but put them in a room with native speakers and their macro skills are too undeveloped for them to keep up with casual conversation. In time management, macro skills are the major ones we have already discussed. Organization, prioritization, and routine are all macro skills. These skills can be applied to small scale situations as well, in the form of micro skills. In this chapter, you will learn step by step how to apply micro time management skills to a meeting. This will both deepen your comprehension of these skills and give you a great way to practice them.

I used to dread meetings. It was so annoying to have to schedule them. When I worked from home it was even worse, because my kids were always a distraction. I ended up talking to my manager about how I was feeling. I told him about my desire to increase my productivity, and that I was dragging my feet to meetings because of it. I brought up some of the time management strategies that I had come up with, and he liked them. We worked on developing them for groups rather than just myself. We eventually presented it to the rest of the office, and everyone else really liked it as well! Turns out I wasn't alone in hating meetings. We worked to develop understanding, so that everyone in the room was on the same page and had the same goals when it came to meetings. This mutual understanding made it so everyone in the room felt included; like they had a voice. The office is a lot friendlier to be in now, and our meetings are much more efficient. Here's how we did it.

The first thing you should do in your meetings is prioritize and make a to do list, just like you do for your work week. This can be done in the form of a meeting agenda ahead of time. Doing it in person takes longer, but it boosts the communications skills and mutual understanding of all the participants. A person of seniority can manage this part, and the agenda should be visible in some way throughout the whole meeting. The agenda should include goals as well. When you state the goals of the meeting clearly from the start, it's much easier for the participants to stay focused on what you are trying to accomplish.

Throughout this process, it's good to keep your whole team informed on what your goals are. Not only for the meeting, but for your productivity improvements as well. Again, mutual understanding is incredibly beneficial for a team. When everyone is on the same page, they can all begin to understand the meanings behind the goals you have set out. Now, instead of a tangle of understandings and ideas, you can move forward with clarity and speed.

Making goals for a team seems different than making goals for yourself, but there are more similarities than differences. Team goals can be work oriented, just like your own. This includes assigning project due dates, for example. But, just like on your own, group goals can be growth oriented, too. Growth oriented goals can be things like improving group harmony, improving conversation skills, or learning how to help each other learn. These goals are just as important as the work oriented ones. You're very likely already familiar with those. The growth oriented ones are more difficult to implement. Try to talk with your coworkers directly about how you want to grow as a team.

Team growth is shown through more efficient meetings, ease of understanding, and developing common language. For example, say you want to talk to your team about increasing productivity. If you simply say this, you probably won't have explained it well enough for everyone to understand, much less for them to all be on the same page. You could take it a step further. You explain your definition of productivity, give a few examples, and then assume you did your job. That's great, but if you want the whole group to have a common understanding of what productivity is, you need to have a conversation about what it looks like.

Instead of a presentation, you can have an open discussion where everyone shares what productivity means to them, how they can increase their personal productivity, how the group can increase its productivity, and what the end goal looks like. This way, everyone at the table has the same goal and the same understanding of that goal. You don't usually have to have these conversations with yourself, simply because you are thinking your own thoughts. But everyone thinks differently, so establishing group understanding takes the execution of a project from good enough to incredible.

Once you have your goals and agenda ready, you can start your meeting. Don't let distractions or time wasters get in the way of productivity. These include small talk, idle commentary, and repetition. There are a few methods you can employ to avoid these disturbances. Small talk is okay at the start of a meeting, but you should work to tone it down once the meeting has begun. Ask people to arrive early so that they can catch up with each other without eating into the meeting time. Idle commentary is present at all meetings, but it's avoidable. Idle commentary occurs when people are adding things to the conversation that don't help the team move forward. Some of your team members may have trouble in meetings with coming up with unique remarks, but they still want their voices heard. Because of this, they may start to fill meetings with conversational fluff. Repeating previously stated ideas, rephrasing what others say, and evaluating the ideas of others are all examples of this idle talk. If you notice it happening in your meetings, you can try to have control over it in a few different ways.

First, you can make the agenda more detailed and even add times to the different topics. Adding a sense of urgency to the meeting can put pressure on the members to move along from topic to topic, instead of idling on one specific point. You can also create this effect by shortening the meeting time. The reduced time slot will also create time pressure. If the time approach doesn't work, and you notice that a member of your team is offering only idle talk, you can speak to the group as a whole or pull that person aside for a conversation about quality over quantity.

We all had those unfortunate debate days in high school where we were graded on how many times we talked instead of the content of our comments. In the workplace, that approach is completely unnecessary. Discuss how you value unique ideas. Acknowledge that if someone isn't talking as much, their silence is not a reflection of their capabilities. Some people simply take more time to form ideas than others. Be open with your team. Eliminate quantity as a tool of competition in your meetings, and they'll become much more productive.

You may also have trouble with wasting time when the entire team is doing these unhelpful conversational distractions. Meetings that last longer than 45 minutes are especially susceptible to this. If your meeting needs to be longer, then plan for a short break. Have a spot where you can take five and stretch, stop talking about the topics at hand, have some water and reset your minds. Breaks are important and meetings need them, too.

Your meetings may seem stretched and inefficient even when everyone is participating at their fullest. This could be caused by the time frame of the meeting itself. Sit down after your meeting and reflect. What time did everyone arrive? What time did you start talking about the topics at hand? What time did you finish the agenda? What time did everyone leave? Observe these times in your next meeting. You probably aren't starting your meetings as precisely on time as you thought you were. There's also very likely a large gap between finishing the agenda and actually leaving the meeting. These two end up merging together so that you are spending much more time in these meetings than you actually have to. You should establish the expectation that meetings start and end at specific times. Precision in scheduling is a great way to boost your productivity. Your coworkers will also benefit from a reduction in time wasted.

You can cut down on idle time in a few ways. First, the start and end times of the meeting should be precise and emphasized before the meeting begins. Encourage people to follow them specifically. Next, teach people how to always be on time. The golden rule of time management is this: if you're on time, you're late, and if you're five minutes early, you're on time. When your team learns to follow this rule, it will be much easier to actually start on time. As a bonus, when everyone is early, small talk starts and ends before the meeting does. Your ending time should also be strict. If you end a meeting on time and then spend twenty minutes discussing in the hallway, you didn't truly end the meeting. If you notice that people tend to idle after the meeting and talk more, you may need to simply make the meetings longer. Try to encourage disbursement after the meeting. You are blocking your time so that most minutes of the work day have a specific task assigned to them. If your meetings consistently run late, you can't efficiently make those blocks.

Meetings can waste time in many ways, but one that is more subtle is also complex to handle. Your meetings may be inefficient if you are inviting the wrong people. Too many, too few, or too different voices can all contribute to prolonged discussions that aren't actually productive. You don't need to invite the lead generators to sales meetings. You don't need 500 people in an online meeting when most are just going to read the summary email anyway. With a good note taker, you can invite a team's supervisor instead of the whole team. Before you send out meeting invites, you need to reflect on which voices in that room are necessary and which just fill space. This is a difficult and sometimes harsh task. While some would appreciate going to fewer meetings, many people may feel left out when they aren't included. This is why communication in the workplace is paramount. If you can convey to your whole team that you need all of your meetings to be as efficient as possible, you can explain why meetings have lower attendance numbers. All the voices in your office are important. Some simply need to be heard at different times than others.

The biggest way to improve meetings is to stay on topic. Focus is an incredibly important skill. As you work to improve your time management skills, you've probably already noticed just how important focus and concentration are. The whole point of blocking time and deep work are just that: maintaining focus. So, if you've tried all the above methods to help your meetings move better and you feel like you still aren't seeing results, your team may just need a dose of concentration. If you can, you should have days that are specifically for meetings and days where meetings aren't allowed. When you do this, you are structuring the week around these big communication sessions. Now, no one in your meetings will be stressed about the emails they need to get to or phone calls they need to return. Everyone knows that today is a meeting day and people are harder to reach. This clears the clutter of the minds of your team members so they can let themselves be in the moment.

You can also encourage focus by reducing small distractions. Ask that phones be turned off or remain on silent during meetings. Have the windows closed so people can't zone out looking at them. Don't use flashy imagery on your PowerPoints and other presentation materials. This approach may make meetings sound dull, but if you invited the right people and the meeting is the correct length, there won't be an opportunity for people to feel bored. When you do notice people zoning out, that's a good indicator that you should take a break. Everyone has a different attention span and different attention needs. If someone needs to stand up more often, or doodle to pay attention, let them. As long as the rest of the team is focused, these things aren't distractions.

The skills you learn when trying to manage your meetings will extend to your day to day life easily. When you spend time teaching others to concentrate, you'll be teaching yourself as well. Identifying idle conversation will help you realize when you are using it. Goal setting for a group is the same as goal setting on your own, just with more back and forth. You should strive to apply these methods to your meetings. Even if you feel like your meetings are efficient enough, you may simply be used to them being inefficient. You'd be surprised how much fat you can trim.

Of course, in this journey, you don't want to seem like a control freak. It's not fun to be labeled as the strict one in the office. This is why I emphasize communication so much. Share your efficiency goals with your team. If you aren't in a leadership position, share them with your supervisor. Communicate to the other people in your office why efficiency is important to you. Sell them on it, and then they will be much more willing to participate in these methods. Once they see how well they work, they'll probably be more than willing to continue them without you asking.

You've now learned how to implement time management methods on a small scale. How do you implement them in an unwelcoming environment? How do you focus and manage tasks and block time in a place that seems to thrive on the opposite? In the next chapter, you'll learn how to find focus out in a chaotic place.

Chapter 5: Maintaining Focus in Chaos

Chaos can come from all angles. It can come from your coworkers. It can come from your work. It can come from your boss. It can come from your own home. It can even come from your own mind. All these time management skills require you to pay attention. You're going to need to focus as you make your lists and blocks, as you plan your routines and reflect on your day. It's easy to focus when there's nothing grabbing at your attention, but what about when there is? How do you stay focused when there are a million distractions all around you? What if it's your mind that's chaotic, instead of the environment around you?

When I was in college, saying I was surrounded by chaos was an understatement. I had three roommates, a room smaller than my parent's garage, freedom, and a course load bigger than anything I had seen in high school. It seemed impossible to stay focused on homework. The first thing I learned how to do was find a focusing place. For me, it was the third floor of the library, at a desk facing the window. The space had just enough chatter to keep my mind engaged, and I could sit down and study without losing attention. Any time I wanted to study for an important test, I would find that desk and study for hours. I'd take breaks and sometimes get distracted by my phone, but most of the time I actually did what I went there to do. I couldn't replicate this focus anywhere else. Not my dorm, not the cafeteria, not the coffee shop. What was it about that library spot that worked so well? By the end of that year, I figured out the real reason. I had made it a habit to study there. I had trained myself.

Our brains are capable of being trained in incredible ways. When you study in the same place every time, you build something called context matching (Imundo, 2019). This is a process in which your brain associates a place with other information. You should already be familiar with this. Maybe walking into your childhood home brings back forgotten memories. A certain smell could remind you of a different time. Listening to a song can bring us back to the time we first heard it. Context matching is a powerful tool we rarely realize we have. By studying in the same place every time I needed to, I was training my brain that "library = focus." Once I had established the context, simply going to the library told my brain to go into focusing mode.

If you are having trouble focusing, the first thing you should do is make your own library spot. It can be your desk at work or at home. It doesn't need to be anything fancy. When you get to your spot, think actively about your goals, activities, schedule and to do list. Focus on focusing. You only need to do this for a couple minutes. It will jog your brain so that the first thing you are thinking about when you arrive is focus. After a few weeks of this, you'll have adjusted your thinking to associate the context of your work spot with concentration.

Once you have established your focus spot, you should find that it's easier to put your brain into thinking mode. It may even be easier to get into a deep work mindset. But this doesn't mean you have eliminated all sources of chaos around you. Noisy coworkers, pestering notifications, or even your own stress and anxiety are all agents of chaos.

Whatever is causing the clutter, it is understandably hard to even start focusing if you can't control these barriers. To control this, start by identifying the sources of chaos around you. Use your self-awareness skills to try and hone in on what is truly making you break your attention. Make a list of what these things are. Categorize them as controllable and non-controllable. Controllable chaos is internal or external, but it can be eliminated or mitigated by direct action. Non-controllable chaos can also be external or internal, but you can't directly control it. For example, ceaseless email notifications are a controllable chaos source. You can mute your emails for specific times, set an away message, and block out time in your day for answering them. Noise from the construction across the street is uncontrollable. You can take action to reduce noise on your end, but the noise isn't going to go away because of anything you do.

Once you have your list and categories, you can go about organizing chaos. Start by controlling the controllable things. Reduce notifications, block your time, and set priorities. The specific solutions are mostly on a case by case basis. Everyone is different, and what is control for you may be chaos for someone else. Uncontrollable chaos, on the other hand, tends to lean towards the universal. One of the most common types is noise. Working in an office, you'll be exposed to tons of extra, chaotic noise that's hard to deal with. The easiest solution is to wear headphones. It's not rude; it's a sign that you're doubling down on focusing at work. If you're concerned that it will look rude, you can talk to your supervisor, but since you're here to learn about proper time management, you can be trusted to not use headphones as an excuse to procrastinate.

When you use headphones, make sure to avoid multitasking. Use music that doesn't have lyrics. Don't listen to podcasts and interviews. You can also use online sound mixers in place of music for some ambiance. There are some that let you mix and match noises so you can simulate a rainy coffee shop, a low energy jazz cafe, or even the deck of a spaceship. Do some experimenting to find what works best for you. You can even just plug in your headphones and turn on white noise or noise cancellation. Self-awareness is key here, as it is in other chapters.

Another common source of chaos stems from motion around you. Physical motion, such as people walking in hallways or trees swaying in windows can catch your eye and tug at your focus. This is the more obvious source of motion. This uncontrollable chaos is everywhere. You may have access to a cubicle or a desk that shades your view of others. If you don't, you can put attention grabbing things on your own desk or monitor. This will help center your eyes on your work, so you are less likely to look around at motion. Intangible motion is less identifiable, but just as much a source of chaos in our lives.

Intangible motion is expectations from your coworkers and supervisors that pull your goals in different directions. It's current events that make your attention lean and sway under their weight. It's your family and their needs coinciding or conflicting with your work life. These elements of chaos can be sources of strife if we don't properly manage them. When I was in school, I had a lot of trouble with this, without even knowing what was causing the issues. I would have trouble focusing if I had plans for the weekend. It was hard to study when I heard about upsetting current events. I didn't learn how to control these things until I had a family and a career.

While most of this type of motion is uncontrollable, your reactions to them are yours to decide. This is where your self-awareness skills will be tested the most. There are some questions to ask yourself when you feel like you're controlled for chaos and yet you still feel chaotic. How are the people in my life treating me? What is my attitude toward my coworkers? Is my family life stable? How do my emotions change when I am at home versus at work?

These questions are hard to answer. Sometimes, it's more important to try to find the answer than to actually answer them. This is one of the most difficult skills I am asking you to develop in this book. If you practice it, you will be able to control the chaos you face day to day. I'll admit, I haven't even perfected these skills, but it's not about perfection, it's about making an effort. If you ever feel lost or overwhelmed when you practice this, reach out to coworkers, friends, and family. Teach them how to control the intangible motion in their lives and talk about it together. Reflect on your performance and try to find areas to grow. You are far from the only person in your life who would benefit from developing these skills.

Finally, in trying to control chaos in your life, turn your attention to your home. You, like a growing portion of the workforce, may work from home, either a few days a month or permanently. The methods from earlier in the chapter can apply here, too. Establish a home office or workspace. Have a corner of the house that is dedicated to working. Try not to share your workspace with your bedroom. If you don't have the space to avoid working in your bedroom that's okay, but it's very hard to avoid procrastination when your bed is just a few steps away.

If you don't have a home office, try to have a desk that faces away from your bed. Never work in your bed. Don't sit on it, don't lie on it and definitely do *not* get under the covers. That is just asking to lose focus. Establish your focus context in your home. Work from the same place every day. Additionally, try to hold yourself to a routine as though you were commuting to a job. You can sleep in a little, but still wake up with an alarm, go through your morning routine, dress with a dress code, and be at your desk at a set time. Your attitude around working will be much more grounded when you maintain a routine.

Apply the same methods to controlled and uncontrolled chaos in your home that you would in an office. If you're like me and you have kids, this is much easier said than done. As a mother, I block my day assuming that I will lose time here and there from looking after my kids. I have to overestimate my time much more than when I didn't have them. Some solutions work for me that won't work for other parents, but they could still help you brainstorm. My office doubles as a playroom for my kids. In front of my desk is a child sized one where they can do arts and crafts, play board games, and watch cartoons. Since they are in the same room as me, not only can I keep an eye on them, but I can see when they are getting bored and help them to switch activities to stay entertained. This way, I control when I get up and help them play, they don't. I also plan breaks in my day for physical activity with the kids. We go on walks, play hide and seek, use the inflatable pool in the backyard, and have fun dancing sessions. This tires them out. It keeps me active too, but the main benefit is that they aren't jumping around begging to play while I'm working. *Most of the time.* Sometimes they do have excess energy and they're more chaotic than normal, but since I plan child care time into my day, it doesn't harm my expected productivity. Some days my productivity appears to be lower than my peers, but I have the self-acceptance to know that taking care of my kids is not a lack of productivity, it is actually just being productive in a different aspect of my life.

Chaos is understandably hard to deal with. When you use these methods, you may find there is still distracting chaos in your life that undermines your attempts to manage your time. Talk to the people around you and ask them for their help. Asking for help is a tool that we all have, but one that very few of us even know that we can use, or feel like we should. Ask family members, coworkers and supervisors for help if you are feeling overwhelmed. Maybe someone can help take on your workload. Maybe your spouse can start working from home every once in a while to help with the kids.

Maybe your office can have quiet hours so you can feel more focused at work. Simply asking your friends how they handle chaos can help you find ideas for yourself. Be open with others. Self-awareness helps here, too. If you don't have enough self-awareness, you may struggle to find the right questions to ask in the first place.

Work-life Balance - A Dream or a Reality?

The idea that you cannot balance your work life with your personal or that you need to sacrifice one in order to make the other one feasible, is simply not true. While the idea of devoting yourself so completely to one aspect of life where all others become redundant is rather flawed. With more and more CEO's coming out to reveal that they feel their lives are isolated, the idea that money does not equate to happiness is becoming more apparent.

Similarly, people who want to be stay at home parents or spouses report feeling unsatisfied with their lives. They feel cut out from the professional lives of their family and friends. Essentially, it is difficult to be happy if you either have too much or too little to do. Satisfaction at work is proportional to the amount of responsibility you are given.

But how do you strike a balance between work and your personal life? Do you have to miss your child's school recital to go to work? You value your family the most and this makes you uncomfortable. Similarly, the time you spend at work can take away from the hours you used to devote to your family and friends. You may have started to feel that you have no social life. How do you handle situations like these?

Here are a few helpful tips:

1) **Create Work Boundaries:** No matter how useful you want to be at work, do not take on more responsibility than you can. Even if you feel that taking home that piece of work can help your career, do not make this a regular habit. While you may be pleasing your boss and helping the company, this will come back to affect you later when your workplace assumes that you will always do more work for them. If there is no overtime pay, do not take work home. You are not there to offer free service.

2) **Prioritize Where Necessary:** There is a saying that you should choose the sin you can live with. There will be times when you have to sacrifice either work or your social life for each other. If your child's recital is important to you, then

take the day off and go see them. Similarly you cannot assume that you will never have to stay late at work. Only when it is absolutely necessary, should you select which activity demands your full attention.

3) **Do Not Neglect Personal Care:** The daily stress of performing at work can eventually take its toll on you. Many people stop taking care of themselves in the way that they used to. Women stop wearing makeup, men do not bother to comb their hair. Worst of all, their daily diet takes a plunge. What this leads to are health problems that take away from productivity at work and home. You will no longer have the energy or motivation to lead a normal life. Remember that you are working to increase your quality of life, not ruining your health to achieve it.

4) **Adhere To Strict Time Blocks:** An effective way to create a work-life balance is to construct a time block for that purpose. Separate the times you want to allocate to work and those that are dedicated to your personal life. Do not let them interfere with each other. You may even need to get separate phones for work and home. Only switch on the relevant ones when you are in that phase, leaving reservations for emergencies only.

As you develop self-awareness and time management skills, you may come across the concept of self-care. Self-care is complex and nebulous. If you were to believe social media, it's simply going on a shopping spree and putting on a face mask. Self-care is a complex psychological concept. Later in this book, you'll learn what it truly entails, how to use your time management skills to add it to your day, and why you need to in the first place.

Chapter 6: Win The Battle Over Procrastination and Optimize Your Day

Procrastination is a serious issue that a lot of us struggle with. It can seem impossible to start working on a project, especially if that project is stressful, anxiety-inducing, or just plain uninteresting. We only have so much energy throughout the day, and just like a battery, draining energy means we have fewer tasks we can do before we recharge. If our energy is such a limited resource, why do we still spend it on things that aren't a priority? The psychology of procrastination can be incredibly eye-opening.

Many people consider procrastination a personal failure, chronic laziness, or a simple desire to do "fun" things more often. Procrastination is seen as a choice. Some people who procrastinate see it as that, too. They may consider themselves more efficient, and that they work better when they have time pressure. But in reality, procrastination is a form of self-harm (Lieberman, 2019). Deep down, we put off important tasks with the knowledge that we shouldn't be doing that. It makes us anxious and stressed.

A study on college students found that students who put off assignments to the last minute had worse grades and suffered from more symptoms of mental illnesses (Jaffe, 2013). The psychology of procrastination is relatively new, but some psychologists think that people procrastinate because of their emotional state (Lieberman, 2019). This is another reason why our self-awareness can help us with our time management skills.

When you have an assignment or task you have to do, you have an emotional reaction to it. This could be a positive or negative feeling. For example, you may react with boredom, stress, happiness, or excitement. Sometimes, when your reaction is negative, you unconsciously avoid that task to avoid the resulting emotion. Say you have an assignment at work that involves tons of spreadsheets. Even though you have to do it, if you aren't a fan of spreadsheets, the task could bring up negative emotions. To avoid feeling bad, you do other tasks. Even if the spreadsheets are due soon, you'll redirect your energy to focus on tasks that aren't as urgent. This does work, but temporarily (Jaffe, 2013).

When you first start procrastinating, you alleviate those unwanted feelings. It's rewarding to alleviate a negative feeling, so you keep doing it. But, gradually, the stress and anxiety of not finishing the task builds. You feel the pressure increasing, pushing at your thoughts, and slowly your stress and anxiety reach a peak. As the due date approaches, the stress and anxiety overtake the lack of other negative emotions. You feel overwhelmed, and finish the task as quickly as you can. The quality of your work suffers when you do this. Even if you are turning in your assignment on time, the diminished quality of the work and the emotional toll it takes isn't worth it. Procrastination can temporarily remove negative emotions, but as time passes it has more negatives than positives.

One of the biggest indicators that you are prone to procrastination is fear of failure. This requires a higher level of self-awareness to discover. When you fear failure, you are afraid of the outcomes of your work. Maybe you think you aren't as talented as you actually are. Maybe you are worried that your superiors will be displeased with your work. Fear of failure could stem from grade school stress that's rolled over to your professional life. This takes many forms, but it causes procrastination reliably. You begin to recoil from doing any task that carries a risk of failure. You set the bar too high and consider any imperfection a reflection of your own personal talents.

In reality, failure and mistakes are natural. As you'll learn later in this chapter, fear of failure is normal but completely irrational, and overcoming it is a fundamental key to success.

Procrastination also drains our batteries. Say you need to use your navigation app on your phone to get back to your house after a long day; but you spent that whole day playing games on your phone, and now your phone is almost dead. No matter how much you need to use the navigation, your battery will die while you are on the road, and you can't use your phone again unless you charge it. When we do tasks, we use up some of our energy for the day. We can get some of it back with caffeine or exercise, but for the most part, energy drains and doesn't refill until we get sleep.

Procrastination saps at the energy we have available and spends it on the wrong tasks. This means that controlling procrastination is a key factor of time management. You can sit down, block out your time, and set goals all you want, but if your time isn't actually spent working on important tasks, then when it comes time to do those important tasks, your battery will be empty, and all that work is for naught.

There are several small things you can do to stop procrastinating. Blocking time, to-do lists, prioritizing, and giving yourself breaks are all great ways to help you focus on your tasks. But the best way to learn to stop procrastinating is to develop self-awareness. Your self-awareness can tell you which feelings you are avoiding when you're procrastinating. It will also help you notice you're putting something off in the first place. When you notice you're procrastinating, take a few minutes to ask yourself a few questions. What are you putting off? Why are you avoiding it? How does that task make you feel?

Asking yourself these questions will help you pinpoint why you're procrastinating. If you find out the cause, you can tackle it at the source. Maybe you're experiencing feelings of inadequacy and feel like you'll fail at the task you need to undertake. In that case, you can reach out to friends or your superiors for their unbiased constructive criticism, or you can do a very small task that helps you feel accomplished. If you really are struggling with spreadsheets, you can watch a few tutorials online to better understand what you need to do. As you get more practice, you can address your procrastination tendencies at the source, assuage your fears, and finish what you need to do to stop delaying the inevitable.

One thing that causes procrastination, energy drainage, and wasted time is perfectionism. Striving for perfection is a social norm as well as a personal expectation. In terms of social norms, the expectation of perfection has increased in the last several years (Curran & Hill, 2018). In every category, be it physical looks, academic achievement, social connections, or material possessions, perfectionist ideals are pushing us to increase our expectations for ourselves and others. When you're on a journey of self improvement, you know the most important thing to keep in mind is that progress is not a straight line. You have to make mistakes in order to grow. When you are constantly pressured to make no mistakes, it feels like a failure of your character when you inevitably make a mistake.

People who expect themselves to be perfect are more likely to experience mental health issues such as stress, anxiety, and depression (Good Therapy, 2019). Perfectionism is a common symptom of Obsessive Compulsive Disorder (OCD). It is also correlated with eating disorders and other self-harm symptoms. Perfectionism can manifest in many different ways. One of the ways, which will affect your time management skills the most, is expecting your work output to be perfect. Perfection is literally impossible; no human is perfect, so when you expect that your work will always be flawless, you will always be disappointed.

This expectation can come from many different places, but it has the same results. You feel inadequate, burnt out, and disappointed. You could also fall victim to Imposter Syndrome (Abrams, 2018). This is a mental health issue in which a person believes that they are faking their talents and skills and become afraid that their coworkers "discover" that they are a fraud. Of course, they are not faking their talents, they simply expect themselves to be perfect at all times. The inability to live up to this makes it seem like everyone else is perfect, and you are the only one who isn't. Therefore, it feels like you faked your way to success. Imposter Syndrome is harmful, and perfectionism is a root cause. If your self-awareness is developed enough, you should be able to recognize when feelings of self-doubt are really Imposter Syndrome. Reminding yourself that these feelings are normal is one way to alleviate them. The best way is to eliminate the cause and reduce your perfectionist tendencies.

Perfectionism hurts us because it degrades our mental health, but it can also affect performance directly. When you constantly seek to make your output perfect, you work longer on projects to achieve this impossible goal. You amplify the time it takes to do a task because the bar you've set is too high. Take, for example, writing an essay. If you expect your final essay to be perfect, then you'll never finish writing it. You'll find grammar mistakes, or issues with punctuation, or a plethora of other technical errors. And those are just the objective mistakes.

Subjective perfection is even harder to cope with. Imagine trying to write the perfect sentence. It simply doesn't exist. So now, you're putting all this time and effort into producing something perfect when you will never reach that goal. When do you stop working on the essay? When do you decide that enough is enough? Whatever makes you stop, you'll still feel like you gave up, because you didn't reach your goal of perfection. In reality, no essay, no printed material, no project is perfect. I'm sure you've read a few books in your lifetime that had typos in them. Mistakes are normal.

You cannot make a perfect work. So how do you stop expecting yourself to? The key is to change the way you think about work. You don't have to stop trying, and you certainly don't have to give up high expectations. You need to adjust your idea of what good work actually is. There are a few specific ways you can change your ideas to avoid perfectionism (Good Therapy, 2019). First, stop thinking something is either good or bad. In life, there is no black and white issue. Your work is not either perfect or terrible, it's all on a spectrum. So, try to approach your next project as exactly that. You don't need to be perfect, you just need to be good. Even changing the word in your thoughts will help you readjust to this new way of thinking. Make it your goal to do better on this project than you did on your previous one. Using whatever metric you want, judge yourself based only on your performances in the past.

Now, as you practice and put more time into doing your tasks, you will actually notice your improvements. You'll be constantly raising the bar, but it will never be higher than you can reach. When you use this thought pattern, keep in mind that progress is not a straight line. You may have a project that seems worse than the one before it. Use your self-awareness skills to understand why this happened, learn from it, and try to do better next time. As long as you are making an effort to be better, you are improving.

Another way to stop being a perfectionist is to value mistakes. Mistakes are how we learn. They are essential to our development as people. So, when you make a mistake, embrace it. I learned to embrace mistakes when I was learning my second language. At first, I was too scared to speak the language, even in classroom settings, surrounded by other people who were also learning. I had very poor speaking skills because I could never bring myself to practice. Then, I sat down with a family member whose first language was the one I was trying to learn. Through a long, tiring conversation, we talked together in that language. Even though my grasp on it was basic, we could talk to each other and understand one another. I learned aspects of his personality I would have never seen if we were speaking English. I made a lot of mistakes when I talked, and a few times he had to tell me directly that he couldn't understand what I was trying to say. But my skills developed more in that two hour conversation than they had in half a dozen university classes where I never spoke. When you embrace mistakes, you give yourself the freedom you need to actually learn. You'll progress much faster when you appreciate mistakes.

You should also try to desensitize yourself to making mistakes (Good Therapy, 2019). Make them on purpose for practice. Take a task that isn't too consequential, such as a hobby you want to try, and don't make your full effort. For example, if you are trying to learn to sing or play an instrument, don't put a lot of effort into getting notes right. Get some wrong on purpose to see what it sounds like. If you're learning to sew, make a giant stitch right through your project and then learn to undo it. If you're learning to cook, use too much of a certain spice so you know what that tastes like. Make mistakes on purpose. This may seem wasteful at first, but what you are really doing is training yourself to think that mistakes are normal, which is true. If you never practice making mistakes, how could you expect yourself to accept them?

Perfectionism is a detrimental habit. When you're trying to learn to manage your time, it can take you from a task-doer to a procrastinating mess. The aforementioned tools will help you drop your perfectionist attitude, but there's another piece of the optimization puzzle that will help you even more. The 80/20 rule. This is a theory, first thought of in the mid-1800s, that in any given situation, 80% of consequences come from 20% of actions, and vice versa (Kruse, 2016). It means that inputs and outputs are not balanced. In terms of time management, this means that you can do about 80% of your work in 20% of your allotted time, and that the hardest 20% of your work takes 80% of your time. Of course, this is a generalization and not precise or always true, but it is very useful in estimating how much time and effort you actually need to devote to a task.

For example, businesses that generate routine sales are usually much more interested in keeping clients than they are in signing up new ones (Landis, 2019). Therefore, a good business will put much more effort into client retention than they do recruiting. Even if only 20% of the clients are long term, the 80/20 rule tells the company that those people will probably make up 80% of the profits.

When you are deciding how to block out a task, you can use the 80/20 rule to guide your decisions (Azad, 2019). Say you have some more spreadsheets to work on. You can expect to get about 80% of the sheets done in 20% of the time. The hardest 20% of the sheets will take 80% of your time. You should identify which parts of your work are which. Is there complex math that you need to do that will take a lot longer? Is there a data-entry task that will take much less effort but much more time than the other steps? Arrange the task you need to do around these blocks, and do the harder one first. Afterwards, you'll have the challenge out of the way, and the rest of your project will run much more smoothly.

The 80/20 rule is fantastic when applied to creative endeavors as well. Someone who writes a short story shouldn't be spending three hours brainstorming ideas if they only have four hours to work. Instead, spending an hour brainstorming and then the rest of your time writing is a much more efficient approach.

This rule is more of a way of thinking than it is a statistical guide. When you think in terms of this unequal distribution, you value your time differently. A half an hour break for lunch is a lot more free time when you realize you probably only take ten minutes to eat. Using the 80/20 rule should help you make a map of your day. The other tool you need to use when mapping your day is a to-do list.

To-do lists are powerful tools that can help you prioritize and optimize your day. But there is a right and wrong way to make them. If you make them wrong, they are nothing more than a procrastination tool, and can easily reduce your productivity. How do you make a to-do list wrong? First, you might simply have too many things on it. To-do lists and task blocking are separate tools. If you are writing every task you want to do throughout the day on your to-do list, your list is going to end up inefficient. You shouldn't be putting stretching breaks on your list, that can go in your blocks. This issue stems from a failure to prioritize. Your list should only consist of your highest priorities for the day. This way, when you check something off, you have actively relieved yourself of a task. If all of your tasks are on your list, regardless of importance, it's very easy to check off a smaller task just to feel like you've accomplished something, when in reality all you did is use up your valuable time.

You also might be making your to-do list wrong if you prioritize in terms of due dates. When something is due does not always indicate when you should do it. Obviously, if a task is due the next day and you haven't started it, you should make it a priority. But if you're spreading your tasks out in an efficient way, due dates are less important than other factors. The difficulty, time requirements, and impact of a task can bear more weight than simply when it is due. For example, say you have two tasks due at the end of the week. One is a weekly expense report that is routine and almost habitual at this point. The other is a quarterly presentation that affects the budget of your department. The second task is higher priority than the first, even though they are both due at the same time.

You can figure out whether a due date is more important by asking a simple question. If this assignment is finished late, what will happen? If the answer is that you simply turn it in late, then the due date is not very concerning. If the effects affect you or your coworkers in a negative way, that is much more impactful. Your to-do list should reflect these impacts before it reflects due dates. If you find yourself needing an efficient way to track both priorities and due dates, use a detailed calendar for dates, and have a separate list for when you will do each task.

Perfectionism can also hurt your ability to complete a to-do list. There are several ways this may happen. A to-do list is supposed to relieve your stress, but if you are agonizing over completing every task, this could backfire. Instead of helping you prioritize, you start focusing on each individual task throughout the day, needing each and every one to come out perfect. Your perfectionism could prevent you from finishing even the first task on your list. Finishing it and moving on would once again feel like giving up. To-do lists are meant to help you keep momentum. When you use perfectionism to drive your day, your momentum will never build up. All it will do is steadily decline as you stare at your ever growing list of tasks.

Your list will suffer from perfectionism directed outward as well. When you constantly compare yourself to others, you can't gauge your true efficiency. If you are trying to count the tasks that your peers are completing, you are drawing focus away from your list and onto theirs. You start to fixate on how little you are doing compared to someone else. The stress and anxiety that stems from this means it will be even harder to accomplish your own tasks, making you feel even more guilty. You can spiral into procrastination when you do this. There are two things wrong with this attitude. First, you can't compare yourself to anyone but your past self. Everyone is different. If you hold yourself to someone else's standard, you'll never reach it. Second, when you compare yourself to others like this, you are assuming that they are perfect and you are not. No one is perfect. Your coworkers are just as imperfect as you are. You all make mistakes. Do your best to forget what the people around you are doing. Do not let the outside world change what you put on your own to-do list. It's the best way to make an ineffective list.

Failing to accomplish everything on your list can be very upsetting. Even if you aren't expecting perfection, missing out on one or two tasks can feel like you lost a game against yourself. To-do lists should be a way to optimize your time, so if you don't finish it, it can seem like you are running at suboptimal levels. This may, in fact, be the case. If you fail to complete your list several times in a row, stop making your list for a few days. Instead, reflect on why you may be failing to do all the tasks you think you should be doing. Maybe you simply put too many tasks on your list. Maybe your mood and mental health haven't been ideal lately, so your efficiency has slowed down. You could even be putting the wrong tasks on your list, prioritizing your schedule incorrectly and leading you to get more tasks done that are less important. Use your self-awareness skills here to evaluate why you aren't meeting the goals on your list. Note the reasons you find, and try to combat them. For example, you can reevaluate what you consider a priority and what is actually a priority. You could put a limit on how many tasks are on your list per day. You could also work with your coworkers or superiors and ask them how they would organize your tasks. However you need to, make sure that you are using self-awareness to identify flaws in your lists.

There are a few key things to focus on when optimizing a to-do list (Kiander, 2012). First, you should try to balance big and small tasks. It's hard to get lots of large tasks done in one day, so a great way to make a list you actually finish is to intersperse your bigger tasks with smaller ones. You could balance putting together a presentation with dusting your desk. Some of these small tasks may be low priority, but when you use them sparingly, they can help you become more motivated to do your high priority tasks. You should also always build flexibility into your lists. This is why you also are blocking out your schedule separately. You can put tasks on your list, and put generalized times to work on them on your blocked schedule. Now, if something comes up or a task takes longer than you expected, you can move the prices around to fit in with your new priorities. Part of flexibility also includes forgiveness. If you simply fail to complete a task that was on your list, try not to stress about it. Move on to a smaller task that is easier to accomplish. Finishing this task will jump start your momentum, letting you forgive yourself for that small hiccup and getting right back on track.

When you blocked your day, you should have made space for breaks. Have things to do in these breaks as well. These are times for you to mentally relax, so it shouldn't be something taxing. Having a task to check off during your break will help you preserve your momentum. One that I really like to use is taking a walk. This can be as small as pacing around my office, or walking the length of a hallway a few times. You don't need to walk a mile every time you stand up. I walk a few hundred steps, check off the task in my to-do list, and feel recharged for my next work block.

If you do all these things and are still feeling overwhelmed by your lists, you may simply have too many things on your plate. Just like we can't expect perfection, we also can't expect ourselves to slow down time in order to do all the things we wish we could do. You may need to consider giving up a hobby or side hustle in order to make your daily load lighter. You can also delegate tasks you don't have time for. Spend extra to hire a cleaner instead of doing chores yourself. Assign different household tasks to different members of the family to take them off your plate. Hire a friend or neighbor to walk your dog. Sharing is caring, and sometimes as adults we forget that lesson. Cutting down on personal responsibilities will make your to-do list much more approachable in the long run.

One trick I love that really helps me get work done is splitting tasks. Say I need to make dinner every night during the week. Instead of making dinner from scratch every night, I prepare a few ingredients in advance. One day, my to-do list will include making five days' worth of rice. Another day it will consist of chopping vegetables and freezing them. I split up the task into smaller pieces, and do each piece on different days. Now, I have the same amount of work, but it feels much easier, and I can get it done with less effort. If you have a large task, try to split it into a few steps. Preparation, execution, and evaluation. For my dinners, I did the preparation early, did the execution—the actual cooking—every night, and did the evaluation—deciding what to make—in one day, usually Sunday. Splitting tasks into these categories not only helps you do them with less effort, it will give you more time to think between steps.

You can also use the 80/20 rule to make your to-do lists (Rampton, 2019). After you've finished adding all your tasks to the list, evaluate which ones are highest and lowest in terms of difficulty and time. According to the 80/20 rule, you'll spend 20% of your time doing 80% of the most difficult tasks. Put those first on your list, and intersperse them with less time consuming tasks to diversify your day. This will also guarantee that you are spending your highest energy times of the day accomplishing the hardest tasks. Using my cooking example, sometimes I just have too much to do and I don't even have time to chop vegetables. Making the dinner is much more valuable to me than chopping up vegetables, so I'll skip chopping and buy pre-chopped vegetables at the grocery store. The 80/20 rule told me that I should be getting 80% of my results from 20% of my time, and chopping vegetables is not a result anywhere near 80%.

Optimizing a to-do list involves correctly identifying priorities, evaluating time needed, and cutting out tasks that hinder your progress. Determining all of these things is much easier when you use the 80/20 rule to guide your decisions. Your priorities are the tasks that take 20% of your time but give you 80% of your results. You can estimate your time needed based on previous days' tasks, and then block out time using this ratio. Then, you can eliminate time-wasting tasks by finding the ones that take 80% of your time but only return 20% of your results. Refining this skill will take lots of trial and error, so, just like with work, expect to make mistakes.

In your effort to manage your time better, you should make sure you are using what time you have as efficiently as possible. Optimizing your performance will help you do just that. So far, you've learned how to make to-do lists, prioritize tasks, develop self-awareness, routines, and goals. You may now have more questions than answers. I keep telling you that practice is necessary to develop those skills, but how do you actually practice? These skills are pretty reliant on interpersonal interaction and a day-to-day routine. You should practice using the tools in this chapter in a controlled environment, so that when you need to use them in your day-to-day life, you'll already have the skills you need to fine-tune your day.

Chapter 7: The Art of Self Care

Learning to manage your time is fantastic. Multiplying your productivity is wonderful. It makes you feel better about yourself. You gain confidence in your own abilities, but it can't end there. If you're emphasizing your work productivity but pushing aside your own needs and health, you're not helping yourself in the long run. In fact, neglecting your personal needs can hurt you and you can even end up less productive as a result. Marathon runners don't start their race with sprints. They pace themselves, going faster or slower at predetermined points in order to optimize their route. They may even take walking breaks or have sections at a slow jog. Yet they are still running 26.2 miles faster than an untrained person can ever imagine. Pacing is key to true productivity. Once you've learned how to maximize how you use your time, you need to learn how to use what's left.

The first thing you should focus on in terms of your own personal preservation is downtime. You need to learn to use your free time as efficiently as you use your work time. Like all of the previous skills, this will take self-awareness, reflection, and trial and error. Learning how to spend your free time is an invaluable skill that's worth the time it takes. You can learn to optimize your free time in a few ways. First, if you have chores and housework that you can't find time for, and you have the means, hire someone to do them for you. Time is money. If you can spend time doing something relaxing that you are otherwise spending on vacuuming and mowing your lawn, pay someone else to do it. Think of it as buying more time in your day. Of course, if you don't have the means to do this, you'll still need to do your chores, but hiring a cleaner or mower is cheaper than it seems. You could also consider hiring them less frequently. Maybe once a month you can hire a housekeeper instead of once a week. You'll still be saving yourself time, just less.

Your downtime can come from many different sources. Overestimating the time it takes you to do tasks is the first source. All that extra time in your day means it's likely you have more breaks than you thought you would. You should also be blocking in breaks for specific times. Another source is simply your increased productivity. As you learn to work efficiently and develop the skills laid out here, you'll notice you simply complete tasks faster than you used to. Suddenly, you'll have more time in your day to do other things. You can also learn to delegate tasks. You can ask your spouse to share some cleaning or childcare duties that you would usually handle on your own. You can have your kids do chores if they're old enough. Reach out to others to help shoulder your burdens. Downtime also comes from optimizing how you spend your free time. If you spend your free time scrolling through social media, you may feel as though you wasted your break. It can also feel a lot shorter than it really is. Use your downtime to do the things you really want to do. Have a hobby in mind when you start this journey. Have a skill you want to learn or develop, like painting or writing. Your self-satisfaction and confidence will skyrocket when you spend your free time working on a project you love.

Avoid mindless activities. This is another way to make your free time feel empty. Don't just turn on the TV, only to scroll on your phone. Don't turn on a podcast and then immediately zone out. You do need to give yourself brain breaks every once in a while, but you can use your brain breaks to use another part of your body. I like to take walks when I need a break from thinking. I turn on something I like listening to and just walk around the neighborhood. I end up thinking about everything and anything, and sometimes nothing at all. You could also go for a drive. You could even watch a show that holds your attention but is easy to watch, like a sitcom. Brain breaks vary from person to person, but they should always do a few things. First, they should let your mind wander freely. It's likely you won't really remember what you were thinking about specifically, just that you were thinking. Second, it should be relaxing. Introducing stress into your free time isn't helpful and it certainly doesn't balance your lifestyle. You might as well keep working! If you spend your free time doing something frustrating, change the activity.

Finally, the activity should activate your theta brainwaves (Larson, 2020). Your brain operates at different frequencies, measured in Hertz, just like the electricity in your house. There are several different types of brain waves that have different purposes depending on their speed. The faster your brain waves, the more alert and excited you are. The slowest brain waves occur when you are asleep. In between are the theta brain waves. This is also referred to as autopilot. When you're doing something repetitive for a while, such as walking, your brain relaxes into a slower state. This state can boost creativity and relaxation, without you needing to take a nap. When you drive a familiar route, it can sometimes feel like you aren't actually paying attention to the road. This may be because your brain is using theta waves. Walking and repetitive crafts like knitting also activate this. When you go to take a brain break, try to do an activity that makes you feel like you're on autopilot. This is a way to empirically and biologically reset your thinking. You can tell the difference between autopilot and mindless activities through practicing self-awareness.

A mindless activity is usually also body-less. Laying on the couch watching TV is not a brain break. I like to ask myself "Could I take a nap doing this?" If the answer is yes, I'm not taking a theta wave brain break, I'm just relaxing. Relaxing isn't bad, but if you planned a brain break and ended up relaxing, that's not good time management.

Breaks and hobbies are just one way to spend your free time. You also need to utilize self-care. This can be confusing, especially since the popular definition of self-care is not the clinical one. Let's go over exactly what self-care is, what benefits it does and doesn't provide, and how you can use it to optimize your productivity.

Self-care is any activity that you do to promote your own wellbeing (Michael, 2018). This can be physical, mental, or spiritual. Self-care is important in every day-to-day lifestyle. It helps you ground yourself, improve your health, and practice self-awareness. It will also increase your ability to spend your free time wisely. What activities you do when you use self-care vary completely from person to person. Eating healthy and exercising are both forms of self-care, but how you do those things is completely up to you. It is also avoiding activities that you don't like and that harm your health. This book can't prescribe self-care practices to you, but I can help you understand what they look like and what their purpose is.

My first idea of self-care was face masks and movie nights. Skin care is important, but that's such an oversimplification of what the concept of self-care is that it's almost funny. When I set aside time for self-care, I am setting aside time to do things that I know will make me happier and healthier after I do them. I ask myself if I will be happier, or even simply less unhappy, if I do something. If I eat this ice cream, will I improve my life? I'm lactose intolerant so probably not. If I buy this expensive makeup, will that help? I've noticed, through trial and error and self-awareness, that when I wear make up my self-confidence goes up. Staying up until 2:00 a.m. is fun, but on a work night it's not healthy and it's not self-care.

Sit down and have a conversation with yourself in which you reflect on what is and isn't self-care. What actions do you take in your life that can help you feel better? That being said, self-care can also be what you *don't* do. It's taking a brain break instead of a mindless pastime. It's improving your time management skills so you have more free time. Eating healthy is self-care. Exercise is self-care.

Whether or not something is self-care is evaluated by these principles.

You can start your self-care journey like you started your time management journey: with a list. Make a list of activities with two columns: things you *should* do and things you *shouldn't* do. Think throughout your day and regularly add activities to both columns of the list. You don't need to start each of them immediately, but you should, for at least a few weeks, be constantly aware of what you are doing and the impact your activities have on your health. Keep this list accessible and visible at all times. At the end of the week, take extra time to both reflect on what you have added to the list and brainstorm more things to include. Once your list is long enough for your liking, start making those bullet points a habit. This will be very challenging. Forming a habit takes time, discipline, and repetition.

There are a few tricks that I have found to help me solidify my habits. First, I don't pressure myself to make a habit that's complex on the first try. If I want to start exercising more, for example, I don't expect myself to become a bodybuilder overnight. I start by asking myself to make time a few days a week to exercise. If I have a day with more energy, I exercise, but if I'm tired or busy, I don't, and I don't count that as a failure on my part. If you start with your expectations too high, you risk letting yourself down. Defeating your confidence is not useful.

Second, I am always writing my habits down when I'm trying to form them. If I stretch for five minutes, I write it down. If I am too tired to exercise, I write that down. If I walk five miles, I write that down. This helps me to correctly remember how I am performing throughout the week and it makes reflection so much easier. I can also get a clearer picture of what I like and don't like.

Third, I visualize myself doing the activity. Visualization is helpful for when you are feeling hesitant or experiencing self-doubt (Young, 2007). You can picture yourself doing the desired activity and imagine being happy about it. Now, you will go into actually doing it with a positive attitude. This involves more brain training, but setting an expectation of happiness can make you happy. I like to use visualization for healthy eating. I usually crave junk food. When I do, I picture myself cooking and eating something healthy. It helps that cooking is one of my favorite hobbies. I imagine eating the food, and the pride of making something that tastes good. If I really need the motivation I imagine my kids liking it too. Then, my attitude towards healthy food shifts from "I'm not allowed to eat good food" to "I get to eat healthy, tasty food." It's hard to stay out of the kitchen after that.

Finally, I always try to replace my behaviors, not simply stop them. One of my self-care activities is practicing the arts. I like to knit and sew, and when I do, I improve my mental health because I'm engaging in something that boosts my self-confidence. But it's very hard for me to make time for these crafts. Usually, at the end of the day, my only instinct is to turn on the TV and watch a show. I used to feel like I didn't have time to spend on my hobbies. I used to tell myself that all the time, so much so that I was convinced of it. At first, I tried to simply stop watching TV at night. I tried to work longer or take my time sending the kids to bed. I was being inefficient on purpose to avoid a bad habit. Quickly, I got tired of dragging out activities for the sake of avoidance. I started using that time to work on my hobbies. I learned how to replace TV watching with knitting and sewing. Once I did, it felt like I had time in my day again. Some days I'm still too tired to do anything but watch TV, but now when I do it it's a choice, not a habit.

Chapter 8: A Deep Dive into Tips, Tricks and Hacks to Better Time Management

In this chapter, I am going to provide you with a more extensive list of time management hacks that you can try out for yourself. Some of these tactics may be useful to you, while others may not be as relevant. It is important to take all of them into consideration and apply what is necessary to your life.

1. Make Sleep Your New Best Friend

The first aspect of life that people find themselves sacrificing when faced with an overwhelming workload is their sleep. It is possible to grab a sandwich and eat while you work, but sleeping at your desk can be a big no-no. When you have urgent deadlines crawling up your neck, you may feel as if losing a few hours of sleep can make you more productive. But sleep is vital to efficient functioning of the human body. Not only does it boost your energy, it also acts as a good way to improve your mood for the day, reducing stress and energizing the mind. While you can compromise on the hours you spend sleeping once in a while, a regular habit of getting eight hours of sleep a night is healthy for any human adult. Here are the biggest benefits to maintaining a healthy sleep cycle:

Improved Focus: One of the major factors of reduced workplace performance is the inability to focus on daily tasks. A good night's rest can help you to focus better, remove distractions and improve attentiveness.

Reduced Burnouts: Burnouts at work happen to everyone at one point or another. They reduce your ability to perform, increase stress and can make you appear unprofessional. A body that is already tired and not at peak capacity has a higher chance of burning out. However, adequate sleep can reduce the stress associated with common burnouts, thus reducing the chances of an actual burnout occuring in the first place.

Increased Memory: If you find yourself forgetting simple information, or even staring off into space when you are supposed to be working, then a lack of sleep can be the causal factor. A tired brain is simply not as efficient as you want it to be. To better redirect your brain towards increased memory, improved ability to retain information and higher work productivity, ensure that you are getting enough sleep.

Power naps can be a lifesaver if you feel extremely tired but need to invest time into work. Just set your alarm, and sleep anywhere between ten or twenty minutes to improve productivity. Not to be used as an alternative for regular sleep, power naps can help you in a pinch.

2. Wake Up Earlier

The early hours of the morning are potentially the most productive hours of the day. They provide less distraction, improve your focus and encourage higher productivity. When you begin work at a time when you know that no one expects anything from you for the next few hours, you feel less pressure to perform. What happens is that your approach to work becomes more confident and you showcase an investment to work that reflects positively on your job performance. You can achieve the following benefits when you begin work in the early hours:

Create a Successful Start to Your Day: A study at Harvard by professor Teresa M. Amabile and researcher Steven J. Krame revealed that progress at work was the prime motivator behind performance, ranking higher than being recognised for accomplishments. If you start work early, you set the standards for progress at work right at the beginning of the day, leaving room for continued efficiency.

Higher Email Responses: Yesware conducted a study where they analysed more than 500,000 emails that were sent out during the day and discovered something startling. The emails sent out between 6-7 am had higher chances of being responded to than those sent out between 8am - 6pm. The lack of competition for the recipient's attention in the early morning gives them a chance to focus on you.

Improved Work Evaluation: Research in the *Journal of Applied Psychology* revealed that there was a relationship between arriving early to work and positive job evaluations. An employee was considered less conscientious should they turn up late, no matter how good they were at their job.

The early hours of the morning give you more time to also look after your health. During this extra time, you can ensure that you are having a good breakfast before you officially start the day.

3. Assess With a SWOT

Representing 'Strengths, Weaknesses, Opportunities and Threats', a SWOT matrix can be used to assess your personal strengths and weaknesses. With a SWOT you create a graphical representation of exactly what factors contribute to positive developments at work, along with, those that do not. A properly defined SWOT allows you to generate a structured plan where you can analyse the major aspects contributing to your work performance.

So how exactly do you create a SWOT matrix? Your first step is to create a list of environmental factors that contribute to workplace performance. These include both internal and external factors.

Next, analyze the factors you have selected. Place them into broad categories that help you to differentiate between the factors that are productive and those that are not. Further classify them into factors you can control and those you cannot. You can classify these factors any way you like as long as it stays relevant to gauging your workplace performance.

Now, create a quadrant with the four identifiers of SWOT: 'Strengths, Weaknesses, Opportunities and Threats'. The SWOT Matrix is essentially a quadrant where you can place in your relevant factors to create a graphical representation of performance. Place your factors into the relevant quadrants. This matrix then becomes your guide to understanding how you work.

Finally, assess and strategize the matrix. Now that you know which factors affect you and how their interactions can cause dissonance in your life, the time has come to sit down and internalize the information. Work on showcasing the best of you while developing those areas that are lacking.

4. Triage Your Time

Without a doubt, time management requires mental investment. In order to understand how you work with the time you have in the day, you must ask yourself a few important questions. The first step is to analyze which tasks are more important. Creating priorities let's your brain clearly understand what it needs to focus on before it moves on to something else. Once you know what you need to do, the next step is to understand how much time you will need to do it. Depending on that answer, schedule times that allow you to put in your best level of work on a project. Here are a few tactics:

Group Similar Work Together: The brain likes to gather together all the work that it deems as common or similar. You can better remember and focus on associated tasks if you do them sequentially. If you have phone calls to make, or reports to write, try to accomplish those together so as to both complete the tasks, and do each efficiently.

Create a Quick List: There will be times when you feel as if you just cannot do any more work. You may feel spent, or the workload may just be too much. It is at times like these that you must plow through. An easy way to trick yourself into working is by creating a checklist of work that will take a maximum of ten minutes to complete. Finishing this checklist adds to your confidence without making you feel unproductive.

Avoid Multi-Tasking: It is generally believed that the person doing multiple things and getting work done is the working professional we should all aspire to be. However, this cannot be further from the truth. Working on multiple things at the same time actually creates end results that do not necessarily match the standards the an employee may be expected meet. Attention is diverted and the individual finds themselves allocating portions of their brain to a wide range of tasks. What results is a quick draining of mental energy along with the inability to handle each specific task towards their best outcome. Instead, prioritize those tasks that need to be worked on first and complete them systematically. Multi tasking also increases the risks of making simple mistakes.

Incorporate Fun into Work: A major reason that people procrastinate is because they are simply bored of the work that they have been assigned to do. Adding elements that inspire you to perform can help resolve work priorities and improve performance. Something as simple as listening to ambient music while you work, or taking a short break to go on a walk when you feel lethargic can all improve your workplace productivity.

5. Adopt Good Habits

Good habits are the key to professional success. If popular work related magazines and online articles are anything to go by, then the primary difference between a successful and a mundane professional are the habits that they employ in their daily lives. Everything we do in life is habit forming, and by adapting those habits that serve as guidelines to success, we can better ensure that work performance increases and the chances of professional success goes up.

It is generally an accepted view that forming a new habit can take up to twenty-one days of repeatedly doing a certain act. A simple example of this would be to wake up earlier. Even if you want to wake up ten minutes earlier, the first few days of attempting to do so can make you want to sleep in. You feel even more tired.

But as the third week approaches, you can find yourself adjusting to your new routine with relative ease. You need to ensure that there is a balance between how productive you are and how much you accomplish at work. The idea is not to do more work, but rather to accomplish more in an efficient manner. Here are some hacks:

Eliminate the Unnecessary: The first step to focused work is to eliminate anything that is not conducive to completing the actual task. If you find yourself plagued with situations unrelated to the work you are assigned, ignore them. Similarly, if you are the type of person who takes on other people's work, then stop immediately. Completing a colleague's task will only make you shine in their eyes, not the eyes of the management.

Do Challenging Tasks Before Lunch: Working alongside the natural bio-rhythm of the body can help you complete tasks with efficiency. If you are like most people, you can start to feel more tired and not at your best by the time lunch rolls around. Finishing the easier tasks in the morning, when you are at your freshest and best, is a counterintuitive approach to problem solving. Rather, use the mental stimulation and drive to succeed you get in the morning on the challenging tasks, leaving the easier ones to other times of the day, when you are more likely to feel tired.

Plan your projects: Creating strategic guidelines on how you should approach your projects can save a lot of time in the future. Not only do you create a structure for the project, but when you know exactly what it is that you have to do, you can pick tasks and accomplish them. The chances of you forgetting an aspect is greatly reduced and you will feel more motivated to succeed as you see yourself completing the tasks you created the plan for.

Find Gratification Through Work Completion: If you enjoy finishing work, then you are more motivated to succeed. Look for gratification in the tasks you complete. A job well done is its own reward.

By working on these habits that successful people tend to generally have, you can infuse within you the behavior patterns of success.

6. Lose the Dead Weight

For anyone that remembers cramming before a big exam, the more you use your brain, the more tired it is likely to get. Exhaustive thinking actually exacerbates the process, making you feel sleepy and fatigued. This is exactly why you should leave thoughts not conducive to work at home.

When you go to work, you are a professional offering a service the company or organization requires for their continued growth. They invest in you because they see in you the potential to contribute something worthwhile to their environment. That is why it is your responsibility to remove those thought patterns, memories, habits and other factors that can affect your work performance.

Turn off Social Media: A prime example of work distraction includes social media. Spending time on Facebook or Instagram, especially when you have tasks to finish can not only reduce productivity, but also cause problems with your workplace management. There are many companies that for refuse to allow their employees on social media during company time. This can be especially problematic during work at home situations where you are not as closely monitored. It is important to have the internal discipline to log out of all personal social accounts when prioritizing a task. If your job involves using social media, it is critical that you do not engage in personal correspondence during periods of deep work. Other distractions can include gossip, which can occur both offline and online. It is best to limit or completely avoid these kinds of interactions as it only serves to deprive your brain of energy.

If you want to be a powerhouse professional, then you need to keep work as your top priority and minimize any distraction that contributes to exhaustive thinking.

7. Use the Pomodoro Technique

Work can easily overpower the best of us. As our to-do lists pile up, our mental clarity is threatened. The normal reaction is to feel like putting forth our best efforts to lessen the workload is useless. Everyone deserves a break, but with the growing need to increase your earnings no matter what stage of life you are in, those free breaks can become a distant dream.

The truth of the matter however is that no human being can work from morning to night without breaks and still be expected to be the best in their field. The mental fatigue from working constantly can sap your energy, and in worst-case scenarios, leave you feeling as if you cannot maintain a proper diet or regular hygiene. Especially in fields where creativity takes priority, a lack of imagination can be the death bell for your career. This is where the Pomodoro Technique comes in handy.

Developed by entrepreneur Francesco Cirillo in the early 90s, he named the technique based on the timer that was shaped like a tomato, which he used to keep a record of his progress when he was a student at a University. The basic idea is to work for short periods of time, followed by small intervals where you get to take a break.

Not only does this process ensure that you work with devotion, provided you are serious about this method, it also let's your mind relax after a while.

Relevant to gaining mental energy, the Pomodoro technique is a method through which mental distractions can be reduced, focus increased and productivity enhanced.

The usage of the word 'Pomodoro' strictly indicates the timing mechanism used in the technique. From stopwatch apps on your phone to physical alarm clocks, finding a Pomodoro to help you should be easy. However, it is important to remember that the very basis of this technique requires that you work without outside distractions.

The basic steps of using this technique are as follows:

- Pick the task that you want to work on.

- Create time intervals of twenty-five minutes in which you will work, followed by five minutes of rest.

- Set the Pomodoro (or timer) and when it rings, take your break.

It is best to use this method when you are free from outside distractions. While smaller hassles like a chatty colleague can be asked to wait until you are done working, bigger and more urgent problems would need you to halt the Pomodoro technique until you are ready for focused work.

8. Make Your Workstation an Anechoic Chamber

The world of science always offers much in the way of progress, though not always directly. Different people have different styles of working. While the interval based approach seen in the Pomodoro technique is a brilliant way to empower creative minds, not everyone will agree with it.

There are those who may see the act of taking a five minute break by itself as a distraction, and feel unable to return to a focused state should they take one. That in no way implies that the individual is unproductive, but rather than an alternative system may work better for them. For those that want to focus on work and power through creeping deadlines, creating an anechoic chamber might be the best solution.

It is important to remember that you cannot create a chamber like this if you work in a crowded office. The word 'anechoic' by itself, can be broken down to mean 'an-echoic', meaning a room that absorbs sound and is non-echoic.

A term coined by American acoustics expert, Leo Beranek, it was initially used for acoustic chambers, before seeing applications elsewhere. For the work-minded individual who wants to focus on work and nothing else, an anechoic chamber may be the best way to go. By reducing distractions and increasing your efficiency, you become a powerhouse of potential, ready to say goodbye to the old days of being stressed at work. So how exactly do you make an anechoic chamber? Here are the steps:

> **Step 1. Make People Aware:** Since the key to this concept is ensuring that there are no distractions while you work, making sure that people do not disturb you is the first step. If you work from home or remotely, then this may be easier for you. But if you work in an office, it may not be.

Consider getting into a discussion with your colleagues where you encourage them to ask for your help when they need it, while giving you space to complete the tasks you need to do. Also ask them to not make loud noises near your workstation as it can lead to distractions and reduced efficiency.

Step 2. Create a Clutter Free Workstation: You cannot work until you create an environment where you can optimally function. Clear up any mess on your table and add pleasing aesthetics that can keep you focused. An indoor plant or a motivational poster all add extra elements to designed to keep you focused. At this point, also make an effort to remove things you no longer need from your workstation.

Step 3. Eliminate Noise: This can be hard to accomplish, especially if you work in a crowded workplace. Consider getting either noise cancelling headphones or earbuds to keep you focused. Discuss the usage of these devices with your employer so that they are aware of why you may not always be able to hear the phone when someone calls for you.

Step 4. Make Everything Available: From small snacks to a clock that tells you what time it is, ensure that you have everything you need so that you do not feel the need to leave your workstation multiple times.

For those who need to power through work, this process can be a useful approach to increase efficiency and eliminate distractions.

9. Batch and Bundle Your Business

There are fewer ideas worse than leaving every task to the last minute. Doing so makes you feel both overwhelmed and unhappy with the mountain of work in front of you. If you remember that your body's initial reaction to any sort of perceived threat is to either fight it or run away, you may be surprised to know that this psychology extends to job performance as well.

Whether an individual stays to fight or runs away largely depends on the level of the perceived threat and the ability of the person to fight it. Personality also comes into play here as attitudes towards life and thought patterns largely determine how we react to the world around us. For those unable to meet their deadlines, this is even more apparent.

However, the inability to handle a high volume of work mostly reflects discipline issues over an actual incapacity to do the job. This circumstance, unfortunately, places your employer in the uncomfortable position of having to understand why your performance is failing despite your abilities. Luckily, proper work delegation can see you out of this situation.

Instead of working on large tasks at the same time and feeling incapable of dealing with them, break everything down. A mountain is not that hard to climb once you have taken the first few steps to climb it. Similarly, work is not impossible to accomplish if you segment it and focus on smaller chunks, aiming towards overall completion. The key is to not overwhelm yourself. Follow these steps to mitigate a smaller load:

Step 1. Segregate the Workload into Smaller Batches: By creating smaller batches of work, the mind is more capable of finishing those tasks instead of panicking.

Step 2. Delegate Time Responsibly: There is a large difference between working for two hours and work that needs two hours to finish. Recognize the difference and distribute your time such that you accomplish important tasks and diligently work on what you have assigned yourself for a limited time period. When you finish work within your personal deadlines, larger deadlines become more achievable.

Step 3. Creative Work Comes First: Stemming from the fact that each act of thinking adds a layer of fatigue to your mind, it makes sense to accomplish tasks that require imaginative thinking at the start of your day. The mundane tasks that people tend to work on first should be left for later when the mind is tired and the creative juices have stopped flowing.

Step 4. Avoid Multi-Tasking: There is a common perception that multi–taskers are the ones who are good at their job. However, working on too many things is distracting and takes away from giving your best to any specific task. Multi-tasking also ensures stress piles on fast. Instead, focus on distributed work for a more strategic approach.

By dividing work up so that you complete tasks over a segmented period of time, instead of all at once, you become more focused and productive.

10. Set Up A System

For those who are looking to get organized, turning to modern technology may be a simple solution. Long since revered as a way to keep track of work and life balance, people have been using organizers for years. Take a trip to any office supply store and you are bound to come across organizers and diaries of varying designs and layouts.

There is a simple reason behind this – efforts to keep track of your progress generally create motivation and help keep everything you need to accomplish in one place. For the modern employee who doesn't write down their tasks using a pen and paper, both the Internet and mobile phone apps offer alternatives that can make your life easier.

Here is a list of popular web-based apps that are designed to keep your tasks managed online:

Week Plan: A popular tool used to gauge how much work you have for the week, this service helps you keep track of everything you need to do each day of the week. Making changes to your schedule has never been easier, and all you need to do is click on the day of the week to edit. If you want to go for a paid subscription, there are additional features like analytics, subtask managing and sharing with Google Calendar.

Weekis: For a simplistic approach to staying organised, this web based application for work organization gives you the same benefits of Week Plan, but in a simple, minimalist format.

Trello: Primarily a project management tool, the use of the Kanban style list method let's you create productive plans for attaining goals.

The presence of boards, cards and lists gives you space to jot down your ideas. You can even collaborate with your colleagues, create checklists and set deadlines. Additional paid content includes the ability to make large uploads of attachments, save searches and customize your board.

GQueues: Another organization tool, this web application looks very similar to Gmail. Here you can create space to store information on repeated tasks and subtasks. You can also use this platform to collaborate with colleagues. The Personal and Business Paid plans give you the option to incorporate Google Calendar.

Staying organized is a key feature of workplace productivity and web applications are just the tip of the iceberg of what is available on the market.

11. Calendars Can Work Wonders

A time tested tradition, calendars are a great addition to your aresenal. When you are playing with time, it is important to have a tool that works in your favor.

There are hundreds of calendars available both online, as well as, on your phone. Each will allow you to organize how you spend time at work. But how do you best optimize one? Here are some key tips:

Create Reminders. Everything from repeated tasks to due dates can be placed in the calendar. You can also schedule follow-ups and allot time for breaks. Best of all, you can share this information with your colleagues, so that everyone is in the loop on how much work there is to do.

Organize with Color. For an easily identifiable approach to organization, choose colors for different aspects of work.

Meetings could be in blue for example, while deadlines are in red.

Share. The ability to share tasks on the calendar was created as a useful aid to work productivity. Instead of having to explain to each individual exactly what they need to do, ask them to look on the calendar and focus on the task accordingly.

Study Patterns: A common function of calendars many people underestimate is its ability to create a broad picture of your actions. To put it simply, calendars allow for ongoing analytics on work performance. Reviewing your past work, take a look at how long it took you to finish a task and decide whether your performance can be improved on your next project.

Using calendars to improve efficiency is like controlling the time you have. Doing so makes it easy to strategize, act upon and improve your job performance.

12. Reduce Stress With Self-Audits

A growing mountain of tasks can quickly demotivate you and put you under a lot of stress. More often than not, most of us tend to procrastinate in our work. We put things off and try to hurriedly complete them as the deadline approaches. This habit does nothing but leave you in a tight spot.

A simple way to reduce stress is to manage yourself. Conduct self-audits to review your daily and weekly activities so that you can better manage your tasks and your time. Self audits not only help to reduce stress, but they also help you to maintain a balance between life and work. You don't want to be taking a briefcase full of work home with you.

One of the best ways to manage work, is to plan your day and your week ahead of time. Schedule your activities to improve your efficiency and your productivity. Prioritize tasks that need more attention. Once you have set your goals, review your schedule at the end of the day and ask yourself these questions. Have I completed all the tasks for the day? Did I complete them on time? Was I meticulous?

Asking these questions helps you figure out ways to better manage your work. If you haven't completed a task on time, try to find out why you could not do so. Maybe it was because the task was too complex or the time allotted was not enough. In such cases, break down the task into smaller, more realistic activities.

Reviewing your work is the best way to know where you went wrong. When you discover what went wrong, it is easier to avoid these mistakes in the future. This helps you to effectively utilize your time and complete your projects before they pile up.

13. Avoid The Jugglery

Many of us think that the fastest way to get anything done is to multi-task. We want to get everything done as quickly as possible, and the first thing that comes to mind is, why not multi-task?

The human brain is wired in such a way that it is can focus only on one task at a time. Trying to do a number of things at once will affect the performance of your brain and reduce your efficiency.

When you are devoting all your energy towards the completion of a single task, your brain is able to focus better and it is more likely that you will be meticulous in your work. This will avoid any possible errors. Multi-tasking only serves to juggle your focus. You will not be able to concentrate on any one project. Instead, your mind is constantly swinging back and forth like a pendulum, reducing your productivity.

Imagine trying to send e-mails during an important meeting. Where should you direct your focus? Should you pay attention to what's going on in the meeting or composing e-mails? What happens, most likely, is that you will miss a large chunk of the meeting and half your e-mails probably won't even reach the right person. Avoid this from happening. Focus on one task at a time. Get into the mindset that is required of a task and stay in that zone until it is done. Focusing on single tasks will boost your productivity, reducing the likelihood of making mistakes. This is especially true if such tasks require immense focus and attention to detail.

Multi-tasking can give you stress especially if you are trying to get several things done at once and none of them show the desired result. To say that multi-tasking saves time is simply wrong. It aggravates your stress levels, makes it harder to focus, and reduces your overall productivity.

14. Bid Adieu To The Banal

A monotonous life is one that can frustrate an individual to the very core. The same unchanging, uninspiring routine every day can demotivate a person and reduce his or her efficiency. Monotony can lead to procrastination, which in turn, results in poor time management and decreased productivity.

You can manage your time better if you are able to remove a monotonous task and, if possible, automate a few others.

Modify your routine.

A routine can help you lead a very organized and conventional life. While this is not bad, it can definitely make your life seem dull. To make matters worse, it may not be entirely possible to eliminate a routine completely.

However, it is much easier to discover the banal tasks in your routine and remove them or even work around them to better manage your time. Removing monotony can give you flexibility and inspire your creativity. Find out what it is that makes your life so predictable and try to change it. It might be small things like your eating schedule. It could be how you do your tasks at the same time every day. It could even be the way in which you travel to work. These are simple things and easy to change.

If you are tired of your eating schedule, find new places to eat, try out new cuisines or go to lunch with friends. Change how you go about your day doing everything at the same time. Rotate your schedule and make some changes you can live with.

Try out a different route to work. Once in a while it is good to ditch routines and do something out of the ordinary. Repetition makes you bored and impossible for you to look forward to your day with any enthusiasm at all. Having your daily life filled up to the dot with tasks can make you feel like you are stuck in a rut. Scrutinize your life. Find out if all the activities in your schedule are necessary. If not, remove them and space out your day. After all, you got just 16 waking hours and if all of them are crowded with tasks, you will end up dreading every day in front of you.

Automate your daily tasks.

Another way to manage your time more effectively and end monotony is to automate your routine tasks wherever possible. For instance, sorting through e-mails can be time consuming. Luckily, you can get it done in less than 30 minutes by automating it.

E-mail platforms like Outlook have an option you can use to automatically sort your mail into different folders. You can make folders for newsletters, priority e-mails, or personal e-mails. As they arrive, your e-mails will be sorted accordingly, saving you from painstakingly scrolling through them.

Another time-consuming and frustrating task is scheduling appointments that fit into everybody's calendars. This can take hours and you will probably reach the end of your tether. But there is a solution -- make use of online scheduling tools. These tools automatically log in to your schedule and update appointments after checking available time slots. This is ideal because time spent on scheduling can be effectively used to complete other important tasks.

Not all tasks can be automated, however, but automate whatever is possible so that you can use your time productively to manage your most important tasks. Always get rid of banal tasks before they take control of your schedule.

15. Concentrate on Correspondences

One aspect that truly helps with productivity is effective communication. The most common method of correspondence at work is through emails. It's fast and convenient and not as intrusive as calling someone. Plus, you can contact anyone across the world as long as they have an email address.

But when your resources aren't being used appropriately, it could hinder productivity. Leaving your inbox cluttered with unread, unimportant, and spam mails can get in the way of getting your work done. Here are some ways you could manage your emails so that you can make the most of your day.

Allot Dedicated Time For Emails. Instead of constantly checking your emails, dedicate a brief amount of time each day to go through your email program. This way, you can review, reply, or delete unnecessary emails without disturbing your work. However, make sure you don't miss out on replying to important emails that require an immediate response.

Take immediate action. While you're browsing through your emails, make sure you identify which ones can be deleted right away. There's no need for you to keep that task for later when all it needs is a click of a button. Now that you've gotten the unnecessary emails out of the way, you can focus on the important ones.

Organize your emails. This may seem cumbersome, but it hardly takes any time at all. Create categories, labels, and folders within your email program and channel your incoming emails to the respective space. This way, you can easily locate emails, prioritize them, and file them as necessary.

Unsubscribe from Lists. To prevent an onslaught of unnecessary emails or spam mails, make sure you unsubscribe from receiving them. Look for the "unsubscribe" button and you no longer will receive annoying advertisements or newsletters. By following these easy steps, you will be able to organize and effectively use your emails while improving productivity at work.

16. The Road to Success: Delegation and Decentralization

Whether you're a manager at a large corporation or an entrepreneur running your own business, you're looking to expand. Success is often measured in how large your business is. And as your business grows, are you certain you will be able to handle it by yourself?

Delegation can lead you to success.

You may have put your blood, sweat, and tears into your business, but as it begins to grow, you have to admit that you could use some assistance. Handling all tasks on your own will only leave you burned out and incapable of carrying on. To ensure growth, you have to effectively delegate responsibilities.

Delegation can be described as the process of trusting other people to help you complete projects and tasks. When you realize that you alone cannot tackle all projects at hand, you will need assistance. Through delegation, you can train others and impart your expertise. When you have successfully delegated someone, you will notice increased productivity and improved focus and quality.

Increased productivity becomes the most apparent result because now you have more people and more minds working on your business and deliverables. This improves turnaround time and therefore productivity. With more time on your hands, you can focus on other projects or even improve your social life.

Decentralization is especially important if you are a business owner or work in high-level management.

If your business is flourishing, perhaps it is time you focused on management. This is where decentralization comes it. It is defined as a systematic distribution or transfer of authority and decision making power at every management level. This allows all employees at different hierarchies to share authority and have a say in the decision-making.

Decentralization has many advantages. Passing authority at lower levels will allow subordinates to develop trust in higher level management. This will help them develop initiative and motivation. They feel empowered now that they have the liberty and authority to make decisions as well.

With your subordinates participating in decision-making, tasks are handled much more quickly. Now that more minds are working together, you can make faster decisions with a lot more input. Thanks to decentralization, lower-level employees are given the opportunity to demonstrate their abilities as managers and decision-makers. This gives you insight on who is deserving of promotions and other perks. Decentralization allows lower-level employees more freedom and autonomy. This helps facilitate growth, as well as, allows them to take initiative whenever necessary.

With decentralization, employees will come together to ensure goals are met and necessary decisions are taken. This also results in improved creativity among departments.

17. The 3 R's: Rest, Relax, Repeat

Picture your typical workday. You go to work, complete whatever tasks are assigned to you for the day, and then you go back home.

Now, let's take a step back and start from the very beginning of your workday. How do you feel when you wake up? Do you feel tired? Do you feel like you're not getting enough sleep? Do you lay in bed imagining yourself sipping some cocktails on a beach vacation? Or worse, do you lay there wondering if your job is really worth it?

Let's face it, breaks are essential.

More often than not, we find ourselves not being able to unwind. We take on more responsibilities than we should. We find ourselves spending longer hours at work and sleepless nights at home. This is because we have become so involved with our jobs that they never truly leave us.

If you overwork yourself, your body and mind will soon give up on you. And without a functioning body and mind, how do you plan on being a productive member of your workplace?

The key is to not allow yourself to become congested with responsibility. Take time off to breathe and let go of your responsibilities for a while. Your tasks will always be there, but your mental peace can be hard to retrieve once lost.

The key to becoming and remaining a productive employee is to follow the three R's - Rest, Relax, and Repeat. You may be a crucial member of your team, but you are deserving of some personal time where you're not bothered by phone calls, emails, and pesky colleagues. Every six months or at least once a year, make sure you take time off work. You could either stay at home and relax or head to your favorite holiday destination. The idea is for you to unwind, release all that pent-up tension, and return a new person.

Even while at work, you should take short breaks every couple of hours. This gives your mind small distractions so you don't overwork yourself. Repeat your resting and relaxing as many times as necessary so you can continue being creative, productive, and indispensable to your business.

Conclusion

In the hectic schedule of our everyday life, we often forget to pause, take a break, and think. Sometimes we find ourselves drowning. At times we lose hope, we become frustrated and we feel disappointed. All these emotions tend to happen to the best of us.

But the most important thing to remember is that life does not stop when we are overwhelmed. There is a long road ahead. There are always challenges to face. Some may be extremely difficult, others not so much. In all of these situations, it is important to remember some crucial life lessons. These lessons will help you push forward, take the next step, and continue despite the challenges that you have faced and the challenges that lie ahead.

Love Yourself

The first and most important lesson is to love yourself no matter what. Self-loathing can deter you from carrying on with your life. Accepting yourself is the key to happiness. You may have limitations and you may not be perfect, but this is you. Accept yourself for who you are. Aim to become a better version of yourself. The world needs your uniqueness and your quirks. Only a person who has truly accepted themselves can have fulfilling relationships with the people around them. Even amidst challenges, never stop believing in yourself.

Stick to What is Right

Society has defined norms for everyone. You, however, do not have to adhere to these norms. Stick up for what is right. That's what matters. You don't have to live your life in a facade. Discern what's right and what's wrong and live accordingly.

Do Not Let Your Titles and Positions Define You

You may be the CEO of a large corporation or a farmer in a small village, but these positions are not what define you. These positions and titles are what you are in the society. Underneath all of it is your true self. Don't forget to be who you are. Be true to yourself and the essence of you. Ultimately, happiness is found within.

Attitude

Having a positive attitude is essential to staying afloat in a sea of challenges. If you are determined to face your challenges head on, obstacles cannot deter you. Always be positive, always believe in yourself, and always keep hoping. Life can be bleak at times but a strong, healthy attitude can help you stay grounded. Negativity can be your worst enemy. If you easily lose hope and are easily demoralized, moving ahead can be a tough task. You journey in life will not always be smooth. You have to weather storms and you cannot survive without hope and belief.

Focus on the Present

You might have had a tough past. You may be worried about your future. The truth is, you cannot change your past and you cannot predict your future. Worrying about everything can stress you out. Live in the present. Live for the moment. Learn from past experience and do everything you can today to make your future better. This is the only way to be truly happy. Accept you past because it makes you who you are today. Learn to make your peace with whatever happened.

Let Go of Grudges

We humans tend to hold grudges against each other. This is a completely fruitless act. There is nothing you can gain from holding grudges except bitterness. Let them go. Life is short and there is simply no time to waste by being bitter. It affects your progress in life and your relationships as well. Accept the fact that everyone around you is as human as you are. Mistakes happen. Be the bigger person by letting the past be in the past.

Time management is a difficult skill to master. It takes dedication and perseverance to correctly learn to balance your time. With this book, you have learned how to start your time management journey. I can't force you to do any of the practices I've taught you, but it's my hope that you are motivated enough to find the strength to do them. I hope you make your lists, set your goals, learn to focus, organize and take care of yourself. This will transform your life. It will change how you spend your time and how you feel about yourself. You'll be grateful you put in the work.

By now you should know what time management is and what it could look like in your life. You know how to correctly prioritize your tasks. You know why prioritizing is important, and how to identify higher and lower priority projects. You know how to make a to do list, and how to emphasize your priorities on it. You know how to block out your days so that you can plan for everything and anything that the work day can throw at you. You know what the different types of focusing are and how to add time for each into your schedule. You can properly plan for breaks and personal time in your day. You also learned how to build a routine. You know how to start your journey to self-awareness through three layers of understanding. You know why self-awareness is important. It's probably easier to understand the actions of others now, as well. You also learned how to get rid of time-wasting temptations and how to properly set goals for yourself. You know how to provide the most optimal meetings possible through goal setting, time management, and mutual understanding. You can look chaos in the eye and laugh. It holds nothing on you now. You know how to balance chaos at work and at home. You also learned how to take yourself into account as well. You can practice self-care and fit your own health into your list of priorities.

If you went into this book doubting your ability to manage your time, you shouldn't have any more doubts. I've put everything I've learned from my own life here so that you can benefit from these lessons. I wish I had this book with me when I was starting my career and my family. Fortunately, you have this book. You can take what I've taught you and put it into practice. Highlight and reread sections you may need help on. Have your spouse or coworkers read along with you. Share what you've learned here to help even more people get their time back. I'm sure you'll see improvements in your life once you get the hang of these lessons. Remember, practice makes permanent. Reflection is the best tool you have to keep yourself in check. You can reflect with the people you work with, too. Self-help book clubs exist for a reason. It's much easier to hit a goal when you have people supporting you.

I wrote this book because I wanted others to have the same joy and confidence that I do when I go through my daily life. It's truly a privilege to be able to wake up every day, knowing that I have all of my time accounted for. I'm less stressed, less anxious, and I have so much more time in the day. It really feels like my days got longer.

One last thing I want to leave you with is a concept that has always helped me keep moving forward -- the difference between difficult and challenging. I've always used the difference between these two words to help me along in my own life. For me, something is difficult when it is painful and grueling and unpleasant. Chemistry class in college was difficult. Something is difficult when I don't grow from overcoming it and I *just get through it*. It's like trying to sprint through waist deep water—it just doesn't work. Challenging, on the other hand, is more positive. It's hard, and it takes hard work, but it isn't painful. Learning time management was challenging. It was something I could step up to, something I could learn from. A challenge is something you don't just get over, you overcome it. It's my hope that, when you read this book and learn to manage your time, you find it challenging, not difficult. I don't want you to struggle, I want you to fight and succeed. These were the tools I used to do just that. Now, I've passed them onto you.

If you take only one lesson away from this book, I hope it is this: learn to know yourself. A lot of the strategies I've given you here have to do with self-awareness. As you learn more about yourself, you will come to have more confidence. In my self-awareness journey, I learned to balance my daily activities. I learned to communicate better with those around me. I learned how to teach my children better. I learned compassion and assuredness and grace. I hope you can, too. I hope you take the lessons in this book and learn to apply them. I hope you can make your time more and more meaningful, day by day. I hope this book is a diving board for you to jump off of, gracefully falling into a better tomorrow.

References

Abegbuyi, F. (2019, May 2). *Deep Work: The Complete Guide (Including a Step-by-Step Checklist)*. Ambition & Balance. https://doist.com/blog/deep-work/

Adams, R. V., & Blair, E. (2019). Impact of Time Management Behaviors on Undergraduate Engineering Students' Performance. *SAGE Open, 9*(1), 215824401882450. https://doi.org/10.1177/2158244018824506

Cherry, K. (2019, June 14). *Dunning-Kruger Effect: Why Incompetent People Think They Are Superior*. Verywell Mind. https://www.verywellmind.com/an-overview-of-the-dunning-kruger-effect-4160740

Chunn, L. (2017, May 10). *The psychology of the to-do list – why your brain loves ordered tasks*. The Guardian; The Guardian. https://www.theguardian.com/lifeandstyle/2017/may/10/the-psychology-of-the-to-do-list-why-your-brain-loves-ordered-tasks

Imundo, M. (2019, November 2). *Mythbusters: Studying in the same place, at the same time, every day is good for learning*. Psychology In Action. https://www.psychologyinaction.org/psychology-in-action-1/2019/11/2/mythbusters-studying-in-the-same-place-at-the-same-time-every-day-is-good-for-learning

Khan, M., & Nasrullah, S. (2015). *The Impact of Time Management on the Students' Academic Achievements*. ResearchGate. https://www.researchgate.net/publication/313768789_The_Impact_of_Time_Management_on_the_Students%27_Academic_Achievements

Kubu, C., & Machado, A. (2017, June 1). *The Science is Clear: Why Multitasking Doesn't Work*. Health Essentials from Cleveland Clinic;

Health Essentials from Cleveland Clinic.
https://health.clevelandclinic.org/science-clear-multitasking-doesnt-work/

Larson, J. (2020, July 1). *Theta Brain Waves: Frequency, Sleep, Binaural Beats, and More.* Healthline.
https://www.healthline.com/health/theta-waves

Manson, M. (2018, May 3). *The Three Levels of...* Mark Manson; Mark Manson. https://markmanson.net/self-awareness

Masicampo, E. J., & Baumeister, R. F. (2011). Consider it done! Plan making can eliminate the cognitive effects of unfulfilled goals. *Journal of Personality and Social Psychology, 101*(4), 667–683.
https://doi.org/10.1037/a0024192

Messerly, J. (2019, November 3). *Socrates: "I know that I know nothing."* Reason and Meaning.
https://reasonandmeaning.com/2019/11/03/socrates-i-know-that-i-know-nothing/

Michael, R. (2018, July 8). *What Self-Care Is — and What It Isn't.* World of Psychology. https://psychcentral.com/blog/what-self-care-is-and-what-it-isnt-2/

O'Donovan, K. (2013, June 6). *Why To-Do Lists Don't Work (And How to Change That).* Lifehack.
https://www.lifehack.org/articles/productivity/why-lists-dont-work-and-how-change-that.html

Rampton, J. (2019, April 16). *Time Blocking Tips Top Experts and Scientists Use to Increase Productivity*. Entrepreneur.
https://www.entrepreneur.com/article/332290

Riopel, L. (2019, June 14). T*he Importance, Benefits, and Value of Goal Setting.* PositivePsychology.Com.
https://positivepsychology.com/benefits-goal-setting/

Warner, J. (2007, August 29). *Bad Memories Easier to Remember.* WebMD; WebMD. https://www.webmd.com/brain/news/20070829/bad-memories-easier-to-remember

Young, S. H. (2007, August 14). *18 Tricks to Make New Habits Stick.*
Lifehack; Lifehack. https://www.lifehack.org/articles/featured/18-
tricks-to-make-new-habits-stick.html